LATINOS

IN

BÉISBOL

James D. Cockcroft

LATINOS

IN

BÉISBOL

The Hispanic Experience in the Americas

Franklin Watts
A Division of Grolier Publishing
New York—London—Hong Kong—Sydney
Danbury, Connecticut

*For Peter—who brought
baseball back into my life.*

*Photo Credits ©: AP/Wide World Photos: pp. 157, 161 (Carlos Osorio),
173 (Gary Stewart), 178 (Linda Kaye), 182 (John Bazemore); Bettmann
Archive: pp. 31, 88; National Baseball Hall of Fame and Museum, Inc.:
pp. 14, 15, 24, 46, 52, 54, 55, 65, 66, 82, 111, 123, 125; Reuters/Bettmann:
p. 149; Transcendental Graphics: pp. 21, 91, 98, 132, 145; UPI/Bettmann:
cover, pp. 35, 39, 43, 60, 95, 100, 134, 142, 165.*

Library of Congress Cataloging-in-Publication Data
Cockcroft, James D.
    Latinos in béisbol / James D. Cockcroft
    p. cm. — (The Hispanic experience in the Americas)
    Includes bibliographical references (p.   ) and index.
    Summary: Details the history and contributions of Latin American
players in major-league baseball.
    ISBN 0-531-11284-5
    1. Hispanic American baseball players—Biography—Juvenile literature.
2. Baseball players—Latin America—Biography—Juvenile literature. 3.
Baseball—United States—History—Juvenile literature. 4. Baseball—Latin
America—History—Juvenile literature. [1. Baseball—History. 2. Hispanic
Americans—Biography.] I. Title. II. Series.
    GV865.A1C56 1996
    796.357'092'2—dc20
    [B]   96-11276
                                                                  CIP
                                                                   AC

CONTENTS

ACKNOWLEDGMENTS

I extend a very special thanks to John Selfridge of Franklin Watts for his encouragement, good counsel, and help on this book series and this volume. I also thank editors Constance Pohl and Scott Prentzas and the many other people at Franklin Watts who have moved the series along. Scott was especially helpful on this book. I thank Rob Ruck for his careful reading of the manuscript. I owe more than words can express to my sorely missed best friend, the late Hedda Garza, for her great love, laughter, and insightful help on all my writing ventures. Finally, I recognize the real MVPs: librarians and staff people at Ramapo College of New Jersey Library, Glens Falls' Crandall Library, and SUNY-Albany's Library.

PREFACE

Go to any bookstore and the chances are you will find more books on U.S. baseball than on any other topic. Only the cookbooks or travel books shelves might have as many titles.

Yet you will likely not find many books on Latinos in baseball except for an occasional biography of a famous major-league star. This is because the United States' largest emergent minority, soon to outnumber African Americans, has usually been left out of not just baseball books but almost all writings about the history and customs of the United States. In most books, Latinos, people with historical roots in Latin American or other Spanish-speaking cultures, remain an "invisible minority."[1] Despite the scant mention of Latinos in most books about baseball, all U.S. baseball aficionados sooner or later stumble across these startling facts:

- U.S. baseball's racism grew out of larger trends in society and helped reinforce racism at every turn.
- Baseball was not a U.S. invention and had roots in Latin America and other parts of the world.
- Baseball has been more of a national pastime in some Latin American countries than it has ever been in the United States.

- Sportswriters called the arrival of baseball stars from Latin America in the 1960s an "invasion," as if baseball were a uniquely U.S. sport being taken over by outsiders. The truth was that baseball in Latin America had been intertwined with U.S. baseball since the first day a major-league game was played.
- Some dark-skinned Latinos broke the color line in baseball before Jackie Robinson did.
- U.S. organized baseball did not take the national lead in knocking down society's walls of racial segregation and in fact deliberately reinforced racism even *after* Jackie Robinson broke the color line.
- Even today, when Latinos and African Americans are among baseball's most prominent players, baseball officialdom is widely criticized for its failure to pay nonwhites as much as whites or to promote nonwhites into leading positions, and team officials are regularly pilloried for their racist remarks.

Despite all these facts, almost nothing has been written about the Latino baseball experience. So let's sit back, peel away the curtain of secrecy, and take a look at the incredible story of Latinos in Béisbol.

1
uno

"I AM A MAN"

*I have always been convinced that Jackie
Robinson was not the first black man in the
modern major leagues. The Washington
Senators in the mid-thirties and forties were
loaded with Latin players of darker hue, who
because they spoke Spanish got by with it.*
— African-American sports editor Art
   Rust, Jr., of the *Amsterdam News*[1]

*I was branded a Negro in the United States
and had to act accordingly. Everything I did,
including playing ball, was regulated by color.
Here, in Mexico, I am a man.*
— African-American star shortstop
   Willie Wells of the Negro League[2]

When Latino players tried out for major-league teams, the most frequently asked question was neither "Can he hit?" nor "Can he pitch?" but "Can you prove he is white?"

It seems ridiculous now to decide whether a talented player can play in a baseball game on the basis of his skin color. But for at least sixty years that was how things were in U.S. baseball. No matter how much the managers wanted their teams to win, skin color seemed always to be more important than batting averages or ERAs.

Back in 1911, Cincinnati Reds manager Clark Griffith was watching a talented Cuban third baseman named Rafael Almeida try out for the team. Almeida brought along a lesser-known Cuban player, outfielder Armando Marsans, as his interpreter, and he joined Almeida on the field during the tryout. Watching them play, Griffith said, "I like his interpreter better," and the Reds quickly signed both olive-skinned Cubans.

It was a daring move. For as long as most people could remember, U.S. baseball had excluded any player not a "white American," or at least "white." Only a few Latinos and just two African Americans (the brothers Fleetwood and Welday Walker in 1884) had ever played in the official major leagues. That was way back in the days after the Civil War when Reconstruction had opened a few doors for African Americans. But white baseball officials resisted racial integration of "their" sport. After the Union army withdrew its forces from the South in 1877, it did not take long for Reconstruction's civil rights laws to fade away. New Black Codes and Jim Crow laws bound freed slaves to work as sharecroppers for wealthy white landowners, denied black males their newly won right to vote, and legally segregated schools and other public facilities.

Because U.S. baseball had changed so little even during the height of the Reconstruction period, it was not difficult to enforce the seldom broken Jim Crow line barring nonwhites in the late 1880s. Usually it was done secretly through "gentleman's agreements" arrived at by team owners behind the scenes.

In this instance, Cincinnati's management went public by painstakingly collecting documents from Cuba to prove the new players' "whiteness." The city's newspapers reported that these documents and sworn Cuban affidavits showed Almeida and Marsans to be certifiably "two of the purest bars of Castillian soap ever floated to these shores."

The Reds' baseball park was filled to overflowing the day that Almeida and Marsans made their major-league debut. To no one's surprise, someone shouted, "Get that nigger off the field!" This was a phrase well known to baseball fans; it had been made famous back in 1884 by white supremacist Adrian Constantine "Cap" Anson, the greatest white ballplayer of his time and then manager of the Chicago White Stockings. When Anson saw Fleetwood Walker take the field for the Toledo Blue Stockings, he yelled the bigoted phrase and threatened to cancel the game if Walker didn't depart. The Toledo management refused to back down, and the game was played to the delight of black and white fans alike. It was one of the last major-league games in which black players were allowed to participate. Disillusioned, Fleetwood Walker wrote a book in 1908 that noted the nation's "caste spirit" and concluded that the United States offered African Americans "nothing but failure and disappointment."[3]

The appearance of the two Cuban players in 1911 lifted the hopes of some African Americans. One African-American-owned newspaper reported:

Now that the first shock is over it would not be surprising to see a Cuban a few shades darker than Almeida and Marsans ... with a coal-black Cuban on the order of the crack pitcher [José "the Black Diamond"] Méndez, making his debut later on.... It would then be easy for colored players who are citizens of this country.... The only way to distinguish him would be to hear him talk. Until the public got accustomed to seeing native Negroes on big league [teams], the colored players could keep their mouths shut and pass for Cubans.[4]

The Cuban Giants, the first great African-American professional club, pose for a team photo. When baseball's color line began to solidify in the late nineteenth century, dark-skinned Latinos found that the only place for them in the United States was on African-American teams.

The idea of "passing" was very common in those days. African-American baseball players tried various tricks to make themselves "acceptable." In 1885, players on one of the first all-African-American professional teams called themselves the "Cuban Giants." Because so many Cubans and Caribbean and Central American people were of "mixed" descent and consequently less "African-looking," the black players spoke gibberish on the field to pretend they were speaking Spanish. Before long, they were playing with Afro-Cubans who also could not "pass."

Eager to win games, even white owners and managers

of the major-league teams sometimes also tried to "pass" African-American ballplayers off as Cubans, Spaniards, or as Native Americans. In 1901, John McGraw, manager of the Baltimore Orioles, unsuccessfully tried to play African-

American star second baseman Charlie Grant by saying he was a Cherokee Indian named Charlie Tokohama. Chicago's black fans responded so enthusiastically for "Charlie the Chief" that McGraw's ruse was exposed. Other white owners and managers forced McGraw to stop playing Grant. Years later, when Brooklyn Dodgers owner Branch Rickey sent Jackie Robinson out to play in Ebbets Field, he asked community leaders to tone down black fans' response to avoid another "Tokohama" situation (see chapter 4).[5]

Unlike African Americans, Latinos—along with Native-American baseball players like catcher John "Chief" Meyers and outfielder Jim Thorpe (since viewed by many as America's "greatest athlete ever")—were allowed to play because they were viewed as "foreigners" and "exotic."[6] John "Bud" Fowler, the first African American recruited to a minor-league team in the first flush of Reconstruction in the early 1870s, later recalled: "My skin is against me. If I had been not quite so black, I might have caught on as a Spaniard or something of that kind." In the early 1900s Fowler created the All-American Black Tourists, whose clowning drew enthusiastic crowds. Fowler sadly recognized that "what whites wanted from African American athletes was ... a minstrel-type show."[7]

Skin color remained the key element in hiring decisions until long after World War II. A pecking order remained firmly in place. White Christians were preferentially hired over all others. African Americans and dark-skinned Latinos were completely excluded. Dozens of lighter-skinned Latino stars made it into the big leagues, as well as a roughly equivalent number of Jewish Americans, both groups facing discrimination but at least able to play baseball. Even in 1947 when Jackie Robinson became a Brooklyn Dodger and African Americans and dark-skinned Latinos believed that their hour had arrived, it took a dozen more years and intense public protest before skin color took a back seat to talent.[8]

But knowledgeable fans of the Negro leagues and Latin

American teams knew that African-American and Latino players were some of the greatest of all time, every bit as good as the white stars. That was demonstrated whenever there were games between all-black and all-white teams.

One of the most memorable "interracial" games was played in 1902, pitting Philadelphia's all-black Cuban X Giants against the Philadelphia Athletics in what had been billed as a kind of "racial high noon" in the "city of brotherly love." African-American pitcher Andrew Foster outhurled the leading white pitcher of the time, Rube Waddell, by using his patented strange new pitch that all of a sudden faded away from the batter: the "screwball." After his victory, Foster was nicknamed "Rube" to remind everyone that he, not Waddell, was the number-one pitcher. Two years later, the African-American team Philadelphia Giants went undefeated against several minor-league white teams. In 1906 the talented team challenged the World Series winner to "decide who can play baseball best, the white or black Americans." The white club ignored the invitation.

White baseball managers were annoyed that sometimes the color line barred the way to victory. New York Giants manager John McGraw, for example, was fascinated by "Rube" Foster's many skills. After the "Tokohama" episode, he had no intention of bucking all of U.S. major-league baseball by hiring Foster, but he reportedly persuaded the black pitching ace to teach college-educated Christy Mathewson the screwball. Mastering the new pitch under Foster's tutelage, Mathewson won 34 games, after winning only 14 the previous season.

Foster was not the only dark-skinned player who stimulated several of the new styles of play revolutionizing the sport in the early 1900s. Fans soon also heard rumors that African-American catcher Bruce Petway had taught the famed Chicago Cub catcher Johnny Kling his crouch-and-throw method of cutting down attempted steals. African-Americans players converted bunting and base stealing into fine-tuned arts, including a hit-and-run sacrifice bunt strategized by Foster that moved a fast runner all the way from first base to third.[9]

Foster's power hitter on his 1920s Giants was Cuban home-run great Christóbal Torriente, described by the press as "the Cuban Babe Ruth." Ruth did not like the comparison. During a winter game in Cuba, the Cuban star completely overshadowed "the Bambino" by belting out three home runs. Obviously upset, Ruth decided to pitch against Torriente himself. In his next at bat, Torriente slammed a double off Ruth.

Afterwards, Ruth faced the press. He had little to say about Torriente's exciting play, instead commenting that Torriente was "as black as a ton and a half of coal in a dark cellar." Actually, Torriente was almost as light skinned as Ruth![10]

The racial animosity of many white baseball stars toward darker Latino players intensified whenever they were outplayed by them. Starting in the early 1900s, Cuban victories against white major leaguers reached legendary proportions. In 1908, while the United States carried out a military occupation of Cuba to protect the interests of U.S. banks and sugar companies, U.S. players went to Cuba to bask in the Caribbean sun and make some extra money playing against two Cuban teams: Almendares and Havana.

That year, to the delight of Cuban fans as well as the African Americans playing on the Havana team, the Cubans swept the Cincinnati Reds in 7 of 11 games. The star was Cuban fastball and curveball pitcher José Méndez, nicknamed "the Black Diamond" by John McGraw. Méndez, a twenty-year-old sugarcane cutter, shut the Reds out twice, including a 1-0 near-no-hitter, marred only by a scratch infield single in the ninth inning. The following winter, 1909, Almendares and Havana swept the American League champion Detroit Tigers in seven out of twelve games, including a no-hitter thrown by Eustaquio Pedroza, a Cuban pitcher much less famous than Méndez.

U.S. soldiers temporarily withdrew from Cuba in 1909,

but the Detroit Tigers were determined to return the next winter with a couple of their star players who had missed the 1909 series. This time they brought their famed slugger Sam Crawford. It made no difference. Pedroza no-hit Crawford and the Tigers in an eleven-inning game.

With the series tied at three games apiece, the Tigers finally persuaded the already controversial twenty-three-year-old Ty Cobb to come to Cuba to beef up their line-up. Despite knowing about Cobb's reputation for racism, the Cuban promoters of the Tiger series actually lured Cobb to Havana by paying him a $1,000 bonus to play the last few games. Introduced to the Cuban team's great African-American shortstop, John Henry "Pop" Lloyd (named to the Hall of Fame in 1977), Cobb refused to shake hands.

Cuban fans watched anxiously as Cobb, wearing his patented cleats with sharpened spikes, took off for second base in a steal attempt, obviously determined to cut up Pop Lloyd the way he had done to Philadelphia A's third baseman Frank "Home Run" Baker a year earlier in a much publicized incident. Three successive times Cobb slid with his spiked foot raised toward Lloyd's legs. And three times in a row Lloyd, in one smooth motion, gloved the bullet from Bruce Petway and swept the tag across Cobb's upraised foot, all in one motion. Shouting English curse words, Cobb stormed off the diamond, as Cuban fans laughed, clapped their hands, hooted, and whistled. It was later discovered that Lloyd had armed himself with cast-iron shin guards under his baseball stockings. Lloyd went on to outhit Cobb in the Cuban series, .500 to .370. African-American stars Grant "Home Run" Johnson and catcher Petway also out-hit Cobb. Although the Tigers won the series, seven games to five, Cobb never got over being bested by Lloyd, Johnson, and Petway and vowed he would never again play against blacks. And he never did.[11]

After Cobb and the Tigers left Cuba, the Cuban teams tied the World Series champion Philadelphia Athletics in an eight-game series. American League president Ban

Johnson angrily called a halt to trips to Cuba, fuming "We want no makeshift club calling themselves the Athletics to go to Cuba to be beaten by colored teams."[12]

In 1911, Giants manager McGraw agreed to bring his team to Havana for a series of games. When his team lost the first two games in the series, he tongue-lashed his players: "I didn't come down here to let a lot of coffee-colored Cubans show me up. You've got to either play ball or go home."[13] McGraw's Giants finally took the series against the Cubans. Twice Méndez and Mathewson faced off in exciting pitching duels rarely matched before or since, each winning one.

From 1908 through 1911, white major leaguers won only half their games in Cuba: 32 out of 65 games, one ending in a tie. Méndez garnered eight of the Cuban wins. Years earlier McGraw had stated he would give $50,000 to sign up Cuban pitching great José "the Black Diamond" Méndez and his catcher Miguel "Strike" González—if they had been white.

After the 1911 series, McGraw could not have helped wishing that Méndez had been on his team. Cincinnati had lowered the color line in 1911, and Almeida and Marsans, despite racial heckling, went on to excel. Marsans hit .317 in 1912 and played in more than 655 games for four major-league teams.[14] It was now feasible for other teams to import Cubans, as long as they weren't *too* black! This meant, of course, that men like the exceptionally talented but much darker Black Diamond Méndez were kept out of U.S. big-league ball. Méndez won 44 games and lost only 2 for the Negro-league Cuban Stars in 1909 but was never given a tryout for a major-league team.[16]

Other Cuban players, born with the "luck" of lighter skin tones, were brought into the majors. Outfielder Jacinto "Jack" Calvo and pitcher José Acosta wore Washington Senators uniforms for several years and also played for the Negro leagues. They were the only men to play in both the racially segregated major leagues and the Negro leagues. The Negro leagues never considered any player too light

Havana-born pitcher Dolf Luque was the first Latino to appear in a World Series (1918) and to win 20 major-league games (1923), both with the Cincinnati Reds.

skinned for their teams! In 1920, Acosta struck out Babe Ruth three times in an exhibition game in Cuba.

Even more famous were two other Cuban greats: pitching marvel Adolfo "Dolf" Luque and catcher Strike González. Light-skinned and blue-eyed, Havana-born Dolf Luque heard chants of "Nigger!" during his first game in St. Louis. Luque, who never stopped fighting against baseball's racism, became the first Latino to pitch a major-league shutout and to appear in a World Series—for Cincinnati in 1918, at age twenty-eight, and again in 1919. He was also the first Latino to lead a major league in three areas: shutouts (National League, 1921, 1923, 1925); wins (1923); and ERA (1923, 1925—at age thirty-five). With his sterling down-breaking curveball, the ageless Dolf Luque compiled a 193–179 record in twenty years of major-league ball.

From 1912 to 1939, Miguel González played more than a thousand games for five major-league teams. Called "Mike" by U.S. players, he became the first Latino coach, serving fourteen years in that position for the St. Louis Cardinals. Moreover, he was the first Latino ever to manage a big-league club, leading the Cards for parts of the 1938 and 1940 seasons. He later became a scout in Cuba, coining the now common phrase "Good field, no hit."[16]

After the Cuban Revolution of 1959 and the U.S. break-off in diplomatic relations, "Mike" decided to give up scouting and stay in his homeland. In 1977, the eighty-seven-year-old González died in Havana.

It was never easy for any of the Latinos who first "integrated" U.S. baseball, despite their light skins. Many of them were taunted with nasty remarks and even physical assaults that they never had to face back home. Off the field, they were excluded from restaurants, hotels, and even water coolers restricted to "whites only." Some preferred to play in the Negro leagues, even though the pay was less and travel conditions were abominable. Naturally, if the Latino players were "too black," the Negro leagues were their only chance in U.S. baseball.

For their part, African-American ballplayers found in Cuba and other Latin American nations an atmosphere more racially relaxed than in the United States. For decades, they played professional baseball not only in the U.S. Negro leagues but also "south of the border." As Willie Wells, the great shortstop of the Negro League, once said: "Here, in Mexico, I am a man."

Besides the Cubans, among the fifty or more Latinos who played in the majors prior to Jackie Robinson's arrival in 1947 were two Hall of Famers: pitcher Lefty Gómez and manager Al López. Because their ancestors came from Europe (Spain), they received better treatment than other Latino players.

Born in Rodeo, California, Vernon Louis Gómez was actually half-Irish and half-Spanish. Known as "the Gay Castilian," Gómez was a star from 1930 to 1943, compiling a 189–102 record, baseball's thirteenth highest winning percentage. He played winter ball in Cuba and managed a team there.

Al López was born to a Spanish cigar worker's family in the predominantly Cuban and Latino Ybor City section of Tampa, Florida. As a player, he set a major-league catchers' record of 1,918 games caught. López once called Dolf Luque "perfect in his pitching pattern."[17] López became famous for his sterling seventeen-year career as manager of the Cleveland Indians and Chicago White Sox in the 1950s and 1960s. Before López came on board, these two teams traditionally had been known more for their losing than for their winning, but López turned them completely around. He compiled the fifth best managing average in big league history: .581, with 1,422 games won.

Clark Griffith, the man who first played the two Cubans Almeida and Marsans back in 1911, went on to become owner of the Washington Senators. In 1933 his Senators squared off against the New York Giants in the World Series. Dolf Luque, at the age of forty-three, won the final game for the Giants by shutting out the Senators in

Al López managed teams in the major leagues for seventeen years. As the skipper of the Cleveland Indians and the Chicago White Sox in the 1950s and 1960s, López compiled a .581 winning percentage.

the last four innings. Griffith turned to his longtime friend Joe Cambria, a Greek-American baseball scout who knew some Spanish, and ordered him to go to Cuba immediately and bring back some more Cubans. In the next couple of decades Joe Cambria signed up about 400 Latino players for the Senators and other teams, many of them Cubans. The Cubans even named a cigar after him, "Papa Joe."

There were many outstanding players in the Negro leagues, but Griffith knew that if he wanted to hire good nonwhite players, he would offend fewer club owners and fans if he stayed away from U.S. blacks and stuck with Latinos who might be able to "pass" as white. He hired nineteen Latin Americans between 1939 and 1947.

Extraordinary playing ability was hard to resist. Soon the Latin American imports started looking less white and more black. Sports columnists viewed this as the first crossing of the color line. Red Smith wrote that the man who hired Jackie Robinson, Branch Rickey, told him "that hiring Negroes was nothing new to Clark Griffith. This seems to imply that there was a Senegambian somewhere in the Cuban batpile where Senatorial lumber is seasoned."[18] One "Senegambian" Smith had in mind was Roberto "Bobby" Estalella of the 1935 Washington Senators, whom other players viewed as "black." In nine seasons with three major-league teams, the Cuban infielder and outfielder batted .282.

Another Senators player to break the color line was Alejandro "Patón" Carrasquel, a Venezuelan pitcher spotted by Joe Cambria in Cuba's winter league. From 1939 to 1945, Carrasquel won 50 games and lost 39 for Washington. Carrasquel's Caracas-born nephew, Alfonso "Chico" Carrasquel, became the star shortstop of the 1950s Chicago White Sox. Carrasquel, like Bobby Estalella, suffered constant heckling from fans and opposing players because of his relatively dark skin.

The Washington manager, Bucky Harris, was no help at all. Harris despised his Latino players. "They're trash," he said. "They don't fit. If I have to put up with incompetents, they better at least speak English."[19]

Despite a few darker Latinos slipping under the color barrier, it would be many more years before skin color was no longer a major consideration. Today, we see Latinos in every U.S. team's lineup. Yet U.S. fans might be stunned to learn that for many decades baseball has been "more firmly established as a national sport" in Cuba, the Dominican Republic, Panama, Venezuela, and Japan "than in the United States."[20] Indeed, Latinos have been playing baseball since the days the big leagues were founded—and before. It can fairly be said that the game would never have become what it is without the Latinos in béisbol.

To find out why, we must go back in history and start breaking down the myths that enshroud baseball, making Latinos "invisible" and placing whites on top.

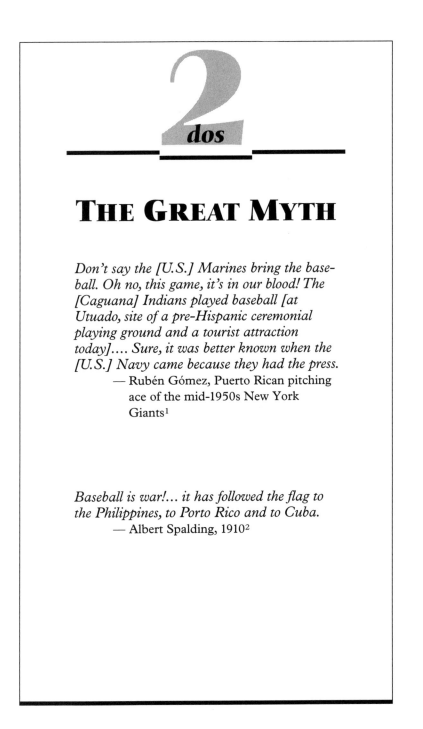

2 *dos*

THE GREAT MYTH

Don't say the [U.S.] Marines bring the baseball. Oh no, this game, it's in our blood! The [Caguana] Indians played baseball [at Utuado, site of a pre-Hispanic ceremonial playing ground and a tourist attraction today].... Sure, it was better known when the [U.S.] Navy came because they had the press.
— Rubén Gómez, Puerto Rican pitching
ace of the mid-1950s New York
Giants[1]

Baseball is war!... it has followed the flag to the Philippines, to Porto Rico and to Cuba.
— Albert Spalding, 1910[2]

A major myth blurring the truth about baseball is the Doubleday-Cooperstown legend. According to this tale, baseball was founded in 1839 by General Abner Doubleday in the rural outpost of Cooperstown, New York, the site of the Hall of Fame. The truth is, "Abner Doubleday didn't invent baseball; baseball invented Abner Doubleday."[3] Doubleday—who died in 1893, not long before the legend was created—was a Civil War hero with little or no interest in baseball.

The main reason for acceptance of this fairy tale was a combination of society's nationalism and racism. It was easy to obscure the truth because baseball's origins were, in fact, hard to pin down.

The Doubleday legend was concocted by millionaire baseball owners in the early 1900s when former big-league ballplayer Albert Spalding, owner of the nation's largest sporting goods business and one of the first presidents of the National League, got together with other wealthy baseball team owners. Wanting to claim the game for whites only, they decided to appoint a commission to determine the "American" character of baseball and settle once and for all the question of baseball's origins.

The issue was by no means trivial. It had a lot to do with U.S. global expansionism at the time, as well as "Latinos in béisbol" and Jim Crow. The United States was shedding its rural, agricultural past to become a predominantly urban, industrialized giant destined, according to President Woodrow Wilson (1916), "to finance the world ... and rule it" with American "spirits and ... minds."[4] President Wilson might have added "baseball bats!"

In the eyes of Spalding and his friends, baseball's origins involved burning issues of national pride and "white supremacy." The United States had just conquered Cuba, Puerto Rico, and the Philippines in the 1898 war against Spain. Not so coincidentally, the year 1898 was when the last known remaining African-American ballplayer was banished from U.S. professional baseball. Three years later,

Luis "Jud" Castro from the South American country of Colombia, played part of the season for the Philadelphia Athletics, the last Latino major leaguer until the Cincinnati experiment of 1911.

U.S. troops occupying Cuba and other Latin American nations in the early 1900s brought back the news that baseball had deep roots "south of the border." Numerous Indian civilizations, such as Cuba's Siboney Indians and Puerto Rico's Caguana Indians, had engaged in forms of ball playing long before Christopher Columbus showed up. The early Cubans called the Siboney game "Batos," because it used a bat and ball. Spalding and his friends learned that different Indian civilizations of Central America and Mexico also had played games with a ball and may have brought them into today's Southwestern United States many years before the English colonists landed at Plymouth Rock.

U.S. historians had already traced baseball's roots to the British children's game called rounders, a phrase still used by the U.S. baseball press in Spalding's time.[5] Originally, little girls, *not* boys, usually played rounders, using a bat and a ball. The British brought rounders over to New England, Venezuela, and other parts of the Americas.[6]

In the early 1900s, Spalding and his millionaire friends viewed the use of the phrase *rounders* as a gratuitous insult to an independent United States of America, then flexing its muscles in a challenge to Europe's domination of the world. The game would have to be clearly defined as "white American." Choosing as the founder of baseball (not rounders) a dead Union Army general, Doubleday, who was already a national hero seemed an ideal way to maintain baseball's whiteness and "American-ness."

And so it was that in 1907 the specially appointed commission handed down its clumsily researched and completely fabricated Doubleday-Cooperstown story. Baseball was now "truly" the "national pastime" of the United States.

At the time the real Abner Doubleday was growing

up, in the 1830s and 1840s, baseball was already being restricted to white males, whether boys or grown men. Upper-class "gentlemen" had decided to make up some new rules, such as three strikes and you're out, or tagging a player out instead of plunking him with the ball as he ran from base to base. These gentlemen decided to reserve baseball for themselves, establishing "clubs" that would meet and play afternoons when hardly any working people could find time to play or attend. Club members looked down on workers as a bunch of "dirty rowdies."[7]

On June 19, 1846, the first recorded baseball game under modern rules was played in Hoboken, New Jersey. Twelve years later, in 1858, baseball players and promoters launched what became known as "organized baseball" by creating the National Association of Base Ball Players (NABBP). Through gentlemen's agreements, they created the color line by restricting membership to whites only.[8]

By 1859, the year when John Brown's band of antislavery rebels raided Harper's Ferry, West Virginia, forty-nine clubs had signed on with the NABBP. The sport became very popular with fans. In 1862 an estimated 40,000 watched a Christmas Day game at Hilton Head, South Carolina, during the area's occupation by the Union Army. The first ballpark was built in Brooklyn that year, with a ten-cent admission charge. Team executives were already seeing dollar signs.

Although still presented to the public as a sport for amateurs, baseball underwent instant professionalization. Teams recruited star players through the payment of salaries or bribes. In 1868 the NABBP set up a system that ranked the teams, with the "upper-class" teams being what we today would call the major leagues.

In 1871 most of the NABBP dissolved into the newly created National Association of Professional Base Ball Players (NA), the country's first major league. Professional U.S. baseball was born. But it was not all-white. In fact, at the very start of the NA, a dark-skinned Latino player was

*A batter heads for first during an 1887 baseball game.
Although the first recorded baseball game under modern rules
was played in New Jersey in 1846, bat-and-ball games were
common in many cultures, including those of Latin America.*

on the field. He was Cuba's Estéban "Steve" Bellán, and
he played outstandingly for the Troy (New York) Haymakers.

Many white racists feared that now that the game was
no longer amateur it would have to obey the new
Fourteenth and Fifteenth Amendments to the U.S.
Constitution and incorporate "any man who could play the
game skillfully, without regard to his 'race, color or previous

condition of servitude.'"[9] But, despite Bellán's presence, white baseball officials steadfastly resisted racial integration of "their" sport. In the eyes of most whites, after all, Bellán was "Spanish," not black!

At around the same time, gambling scandals and contract disputes led to the collapse of this first major league. The NA was replaced by the National League, run by rich capitalists like Chicago's William Hulbert. Hulbert introduced the reserve clause that gave management control over players' contracts and eliminated chances for players to jump to other teams. The reserve clause would last another hundred years! Players were kept under the owner's thumb and made very little money. Hulbert also hiked admission fees.

In 1882–83, two more major leagues appeared on the scene: first the American Association and then the Union Association. The American Association appealed to working-class fans by charging less than half the admission fee of Hulbert's National League. The Union Association gave players a better economic deal by not using a reserve clause. It raided the National and American leagues to obtain some stars but ran out of money and collapsed in 1883. Starting in 1884, Hulbert's National League and the American Association competed in a postseason championship series, the forerunner of the World Series.

An economic recovery from a recession in the mid-1870s created a big demand for more ballplayers. Consequently, some darker-skinned players were allowed to play baseball. Several dark-skinned Latinos and about fifty-five African Americans crossed the color line in the late 1870s and early 1880s to play with white teams, although African Americans (except for the Walkers) were restricted to the minor leagues. Latinos emerged as talented stars. Cuban-American Vincente "Sandy" Nava played for Baltimore and Providence in the mid-1880s before the color line finally excluded him.

White teammates, fans, and newspapers verbally

assaulted Latino and African-American ballplayers. Official Baseball Guides misidentified the Latinos as "Spanish." The word in the Guides for African-American players—"coons"—was less than human.[10]

During the 1880s, club owners imposed a $2,500 cap on all players' salaries, forcing players to launch a union, the Brotherhood of Professional Base Ball Players. It carried out the short-lived Player's League revolt in 1890. The powerful major-league owners swiftly broke the players' union and returned professional baseball to complete owner control.[11]

But owners did not always act in concert. During the baseball war of 1901–1902, breakaway owners founded the American League and raided the National League for top stars. In 1903 the two leagues agreed to a truce and created a National Commission to govern baseball. It was made up of the two leagues' presidents and a chairman elected each year. The World Series soon began on a regular basis. It was a lily-white affair.

In matters of both race and class, baseball reflected society. A nasty campaign against burgeoning labor unions struck at not only ballplayers but all workers. In 1892 armed troops broke the steelworkers union in the bloody Homestead strike. The 1894 Pullman strike of the young railway workers union was similarly smashed. After that, workers in general, including baseball players, went through several decades of owner intimidation and miserably low wages.

As the United States industrialized, some twenty million immigrants from eastern and southern Europe arrived to work the new factories, stores, mines, and farm fields spreading across the land. Hundreds of thousands of the new immigrants came from Mexico; one eighth of the Mexican population had immigrated to the United States by 1930. Because of entrenched racism, Mexican immigrants faced a more hostile welcome than any other group except the Japanese and Chinese.[12]

All the new immigrants were told to "Americanize" or else. A prominent Stanford dean of education proclaimed in 1909:

> *Our task is to break up these [immigrant] groups or settlements, to assimilate and amalgamate these people as a part of our American race, and to implant in their children ... the Anglo-Saxon conception of righteousness, law and order, and our popular government.* [13]

Blacks and Latinos were not included in the push to Americanize. *Anglo-Saxon* meant white, something most of them could never be.

Team owners and the press encouraged the use of baseball to define *American* in a narrow and racist way. The Doubleday-Cooperstown story became a central part of the Americanization campaign for white Anglo-Saxon supremacy.

Immigrant children often found baseball more interesting than school. Although the nation was building new public schools in order to "Americanize" the immigrants, in those days there were no bilingual education programs. Consequently, unable to understand the English language, most immigrants were forced out of school by the third grade. Most of these "push-out" dropouts were able to land a job in the expanding economy because child labor was very common in those days. Many other kids headed for the sandlots, or, if they could afford the price of admission, the ballparks.

Baseball became very popular among immigrants. Second-generation Irishmen like New York Giants manager John McGraw began making a strong impact on the sport, infusing it with a rugged, fiery, and aggressive style of play. Most Irish players, though, in the spirit of the Stanford dean's emphasis on an Anglo-Saxon America, dropped the *O'* or *Mc* prefixes from their names in order to appear English, that is, "American."

As attendance at major-league games doubled to more

U.S. troops arrive in Veracruz, Mexico, in 1914. In the early twentieth century, the United States aggressively expanded its political and economic influence throughout Latin America. Mexico, the Dominican Republic, Haiti, Panama, Nicaragua, and several other Central American countries became reluctant hosts to U.S. soldiers and corporations.

than 6,000 per game by 1910, baseball became immensely profitable. Impressive baseball stadiums were constructed in the early 1910s, including today's Wrigley Field in Chicago, Fenway Park in Boston, and Tiger Stadium in Detroit.

The ideology of white supremacy and the celebration of baseball as uniquely American fit right in with U.S foreign policy at the time. Almost every year after 1898, American Army, Navy, and Marine boys were being sent to the Caribbean Basin to protect the expanding financial interests of U.S. sugar, banana, mining, and banking firms. They secured Panama for the building of the Canal. They landed in Cuba a second and third time, in 1906 and 1912. When Mexico's starving masses rose up in revolution, U.S. troops were sent to Veracruz in 1914 and to northern Mexico in 1916. They hit the shores of Nicaragua in 1909, the Dominican Republic and Haiti in 1916, and several other Central American countries. "Gunboat diplomacy" and "Dollar diplomacy" were converting entire nations into long-lasting economic protectorates.

Latin America soon became an economic bonanza for U.S. baseball owners as well. The one thing the American soldiers landing on Latin America's shores had in common with the people they were shooting was a love of baseball. Almost everywhere they went they were challenged by scrappy Latino sugarcane, banana, oil, or dock workers to play ball. Owners of U.S. companies, hoping to "Americanize" their Latin American workers, sponsored local baseball teams, soon developing the sport into a paid, professional activity.

The history of modern-style baseball in Latin America went back at least to 1866, when Cuban dockworkers played a baseball game against crew members of a U.S. ship in Matanzas Province. Around the same time, a Cuban student, Nemesio Guillot, returned from a private school in the United States with some baseball equipment and taught his friends the game. By 1878 the Liga de Béisbol Profesional Cubana was in business.

The chief promoter of early Cuban baseball was Emilio Sabourín, who, along with Steve Bellán, was one of the island's first star players,. Sabourín was a financial backer of the anti-Spain Cuban revolutionist José Martí, a talented poet and journalist known today as the father of Cuban independence.

Cuban *béisbolistas* backed Martí and his guerrilla rebels, most of whom were runaway slaves and sugarcane cutters. Some ballplayers joined the armed struggle too. To raise money for the freedom fighters, one team, Club Cuba, organized baseball games where spectators passed the hat. Cuban exiles in Tampa and other U.S. cities raised additional monies at baseball games.

As one Cuban sportswriter later recalled: "So many of our patriots were associated with baseball clubs that the Spanish colonial authorities prohibited the game and some principal organizers were arrested and deported to Spain's prisons."[14] In 1895, the year Martí died in battle, the Spaniards threw Sabourín into a dungeon inside the Spanish fortress El Castillo del Hacha in Morocco, where he perished from pneumonia two years later.

By early 1897 the Spaniards were badly beaten on the battlefield by the Cuban guerrilla fighters. When the U.S. battleship *Maine* mysteriously blew up in Havana's presumably safe, tightly guarded harbor in 1898, the United States had a pretext for declaring war against a weakened Spain. President William McKinley turned down a last-minute offer by Spain to cede Cuba and chose to go to war instead.

During the years leading up to the war, Cuban baseball players and promoters helped spread baseball throughout the Caribbean Basin, especially Colombia, the Dominican Republic, Mexico, Nicaragua, Panama, Puerto Rico, and Venezuela. The Cubans became widely known as "the apostles of baseball."

In Puerto Rico students who had studied in the United States, as well as the traveling Cubans, introduced modern baseball. Puerto Rican sugarcane cutters played ball during work breaks and in the dead season after the cane was cut. On January 9, 1898, a game took place between Borinquen (the Indian name for Puerto Rico) and Cuba's famed Almendares team. Twice rained out, the game was finally completed on January 30, with Borinquen victorious by a score of 9-3. Three years later, the *New York Times* reported, "Baseball is becoming a great fad here [in Puerto Rico]."[15]

As early as 1891, Cuban émigrés had formed the first baseball clubs in the Dominican Republic. Dominicans today still talk about how their Nuevo Club and Licey teams won 17 out of 20 games against sailors from U.S. ships that docked there during the summer of 1914.

In those years, baseball was becoming known in Latin America as a "gringo" game. This pleased a U.S. diplomat in the Dominican Republic, who cabled the secretary of state:

> *The American national game of base-ball is being played and supported here with great enthusiasm. The remarkable effect of this outlet for the animal spirits of the young men is that they are leaving the plazas where they were in the habit of congregating and talking revolution and are resorting to the ball fields where they become wildly partizan each for his favorite team.... [Baseball] is a real substitute for the contest in the hillsides with rifles.*[16]

Future Dominican president and world-renowned writer Juan Bosch, a young boy during the U.S. military occupation of 1916–24, saw the two-edged character of U.S. baseball's role. "These games," he wrote, "manifested a form of the people's distaste of the occupation.... The game was seen as [a way] to go beat the North Americans."[17]

One of the greatest baseball players of all time emerged in the Dominican Republic, the superlative hitter Tetelo Vargas. He was kept out of U.S. baseball by the color line. In thirty seasons Vargas won countless honors, including selection to several Negro-leagues' All-Star contests. When he was nearly fifty years old, he won his homeland's 1953 batting championship.

With U.S. influence in Latin America came U.S.-style racial discrimination and puppet dictators who helped crush

*Workers cut sugarcane on a Puerto Rican plantation in 1919.
Laborers such as these spent their free time playing béisbol and
sometimes used games as a cover for political activity.*

strikes against U.S. business interests. Exclusive social and
athletic clubs for well-off white and light-skinned people
screened out blacks, while dictators like the Dominican
Republic's Rafael Trujillo, Cuba's Gerardo Machado and
Fulgencio Batista, and Nicaragua's Somozas kept darker-
skinned workers—and athletes—in line. In the Dominican
Republic, Trujillo encouraged baseball. As one old-timer
recalled, "He knew that it was good for him to have the
people seeing baseball because then they don't pay attention
to politics. Always, the dictatorships do that."[18]

Actually, as Bosch recognized, baseball was a two-
edged sword. In Cuba, for example, those opposing U.S.-
imposed dictators organized student and athletic clubs that

called for an end to tyranny, racism, and poverty. When sugar workers were prohibited from holding political meetings, they would "meet during our baseball games. We'd hold a big game and during it hold our planning meetings."[19]

In the world of Latin American baseball, even those few who knew about the Doubleday myth did not buy the window dressing that went with it. U.S. attempts at imposing racial segregation proved impossible on Latin American ball fields. In fact, African-American players found a haven in the Caribbean Basin, a place where they were welcomed as equals and allowed to show their talents and earn a living. And, of course, white ballplayers too began to travel to "the sunny tropics" in the off-season to earn some money or keep in shape. As U.S. baseball commentator Howard Senzel has observed:

> *Each winter, black and white American baseball players would get to know each other, and play against each other and scout each other, and intermingle in ways that were not permitted in ordinary American life.*[20]

3
tres

JIM CROW

FOREVER?

You [José "the Black Diamond" Méndez] should have gotten this car. You're a better pitcher than I am.

    — Adolfo "Dolf" Luque, great light-
        skinned Cuban pitcher for the
        Cincinnati Reds, pointing to fellow
        Cuban Méndez, an even greater pitch-
        er but one not admitted into major-
        league baseball because of his darker
        skin, at a ceremony in Havana honor-
        ing Luque for his 27–9 season in 1923
        with the Reds[1]

The rise of professional baseball as the national pastime coincided with the rise of modern industry and professionalism in all fields. In law and medicine, just as in baseball, U.S. organizations routinely excluded nonwhites, as well as women and Jews.[2]

The obsession with skin shade was not unique to baseball; it was, in fact, as American as baseball itself. Jim Crow segregation appeared to many Americans to be forever, almost a "natural condition." The virus of racism, an ugly legacy born out of slavery in the South, easily spread its poison to the North. Actually, in the North Jim Crow had a long history. Back in the 1790s and early 1800s, several northern states had stripped free African-American males of their right to vote. In both the North and South, ever since people could remember, Latinos and African Americans had been kept off juries; most hotels, restaurants, and other public facilities were segregated; and special Jim Crow sections of public transport were assigned to "the colored." For Latino and African-American baseball teams playing on the road, this caused many troublesome inconveniences.

But for most Latinos and African Americans, the problems of nonwhite baseball players seemed trivial compared with their own struggles for survival. Because of the rise of the Ku Klux Klan and other white supremacist organizations in the post–Civil War period, African Americans and Latinos felt even more threatened and excluded from "mainstream America" than did recent European immigrants. Lynchings had become all too frequent not just in the South, where blacks were constantly threatened and even a few darker-skinned Italians were lynched, but also in the Southwest, where Mexican Americans and newly arriving Mexican immigrants were frequent lynching victims.[3]

When World War I broke out in Europe in 1914, jobs opened as armaments factories raced into full production to supply the so-called Allies—France, England, and Russia— against Germany. Southern black tenant farmers and sharecroppers responded to labor recruiters urging them to rush

An African-American passenger exits a segregated bus-station waiting room in Mississippi. The exclusion of African-American and dark-skinned Latinos from the U.S. major leagues mirrored the racial segregation in U.S. society.

to northern cities, where jobs were promised. From 1915 on through the 1920s, a million and a half African Americans joined the so-called Great Migration.

In northern urban centers, jobs were indeed available, but skin color determined whether it would be a skilled or unskilled job. There were no official segregation laws in Chicago, New York, and other northern cities, but black people lived in seedy segregated neighborhoods where their children attended virtually all-black, substandard schools. Mexicans and Latinos faced similar conditions.

In 1917 striking Mexican miners in Arizona earning only half what white workers received were rounded up at gunpoint by white lawmen and deputized bigots and dumped in the hot desert—the infamous Bisbee deportations. At the same time, Mexican workers were being imported at a record pace to keep the mines operating, the trains running, and the crops picked during World War I. Yet, because of their frequent strikes for an equal wage, most Mexicans and Mexican Americans were labeled "unpatriotic."

When the United States entered World War I in 1917, W. E. B. DuBois of the National Association for the Advancement of Colored People (NAACP), advised African Americans to volunteer for the armed forces in order to prove their patriotism and courage and, in that way, earn equality. It was impossible advice to follow. African-American men joined the Army and were drafted, but only a few were assigned to combat roles and most of them served with the French Army. In baseball, black fans, deprived of every other form of equality, celebrated when Smokey Joe Williams of the African-American team Lincoln Giants of the Bronx threw a thrilling ten-inning no-hitter against the white National League 1917 champion New York Giants, fanning 20 batters.

After the armistice ending World War I, instead of heroes' welcomes African Americans returning from the war faced violence everywhere. As war plants shut down and unemployment rose, blacks and Latinos were targeted as scapegoats for economic problems. The summer of 1919 would become known as the "Red Summer" because of the blood that stained U.S. streets during race riots. African-American war veterans were attacked in more than two dozen cities by angry mobs of white bigots who did not like the sight of blacks in uniform. Police usually stood by and did nothing. An angry DuBois called for an "unbending battle against the forces of hell in our land."[4]

The slowed-down economy quickly retooled to produce consumer goods. An expanding middle class surrounded itself with washing machines, refrigerators, and automobiles. Few affluent white Americans ever thought about the millions of Latinos and black Americans barely scraping by. At the same time, Mexican Americans, most of them living in the Southwest and southern California, and Puerto Ricans, trickling into New York City, experienced severe discrimination.

During World War I, Congress had passed the Jones Act, making Puerto Ricans citizens of the United States. The Act did not grant them voting privileges but gave them the full "benefit" of being drafted into the U.S. Army to die in Europe's trenches. By 1926 more than 150,000 Puerto Ricans had migrated to the United States, most of them living in East Harlem, New York, as next-door neighbors to African Americans and Jewish and Italian immigrants. They usually found jobs in nonunionized factories and restaurants, their chances improving slightly in direct ratio to the shade of their complexions.

Meanwhile, the Black Sox Scandal, or "Big Fix," erupted in baseball. In 1920 some Chicago White Sox players confessed to having accepted gamblers' bribes to "throw" the 1919 World Series. The scandal created a major crisis for white organized baseball.

Also in 1920, Andrew "Rube" Foster sparked the founding of the Negro National League under largely black ownership. Naturally, the new league owners boasted that

Andrew "Rube" Foster helped found the Negro National League in 1920. Negro leagues gave dark-skinned Latinos an opportunity to play professional baseball in the United States.

their league would be unmarked by scandal. Distressed owners of major-league ball teams quickly huddled. They faced threats on many fronts, including a former rival white league known as the Federal League that had been pushing antitrust suits against the owners' major-league cartel. Moreover, more and more players had been trying to jump from one team to another in quest of better salaries.

The owners agreed on two bold moves. First, they gave the green light to the use of a livelier baseball. To the delight of supporters of all-white baseball, Babe Ruth's home-run production increased fivefold in three years, reaching 59 in 1921. A new white savior was born! Construction of more new stadiums with reachable fences also contributed to the increase in home runs.

Second, in their National Agreement of 1921, the owners decided to appoint a single commissioner of baseball. They made sure he would be a man they could trust: Judge Kenesaw Mountain Landis.

At the outset of his twenty-four-year reign, Commissioner Landis ordered the lifetime banishment of eight players involved in the Black Sox Scandal. Then, in 1922, to help restore order and consolidate white baseball's cartel status, Landis helped obtain an antitrust exemption for organized baseball before the U.S. Supreme Court under the specious argument that baseball is a game and not a business.

Baseball officially became not only "all-white" but also the only sport in the nation to have its own private self-government. As a result, shrewd millionaire owners were able to build up fabulous dynasties, like those of the St. Louis Cardinals and New York Yankees, that dominated the two major leagues from the 1920s until 1946 and 1964, respectively.[5]

Those Latinos denied admission into the white baseball leagues found a warmer reception in the Negro leagues. African-American baseball fans faithfully attended Negro-league games, especially enjoying the contests between all-white teams and all-black teams during the off-seasons when the major- and minor-league teams barnstormed around the nation. Fans cheered the Latino and African-American stars of Negro-league teams when they beat their white opponents.

Commissioner Landis, apparently upset, banned games between major-league teams and Negro-league ones. "Mr. Foster," he said to Rube Foster, "when you beat our teams, it gives us a black eye."[6] But Landis's decision was too costly, and the ringing of cash registers was an important part of the game. In 1923, Landis compromised by banning the wearing of major-league uniforms at the games and by billing them as "all-star" contests instead of "exhibition games."

In 1924, under pressure from anti-immigrant groups known as "nativists," Congress passed a quota system that restricted immigration largely to northwestern Europe, where the majority of people were Protestant. The darker-skinned peoples of the world and Jews were limited to an annual handful.

Jewish Americans, harder to spot because of their white skins, were nevertheless victimized by anti-Semitism. Though as enthralled with baseball as other Americans, they were rarely allowed to become baseball players. In 1920, pioneer automobile manufacturer Henry Ford unfurled a full-scale propaganda campaign against Jews in his newspaper, the *Dearborn Independent*. He published falsified documents attempting to "prove" the far-fetched claim that Jews, the vast majority of whom were impoverished, were devious bankers scheming to take over the world. Most colleges initiated secret quotas to keep Jewish students to a minimum on their campuses.

In the Jewish ghettos of eastern Europe, studying and scholarly achievement had been the values most stressed. But in the Jewish neighborhoods of the Lower East Side, the Bronx, and Brooklyn, young Jewish boys played stickball and considered it a treat to be taken to a major-league stadium to watch the stars play. Eddie Cantor, the famous

Jewish comedian, remembered that when he neglected his studies his grandmother considered it a great insult to scream at him, "'You—you—you baseball player you!...' To the pious people of the ghetto a baseball player was the king of loafers."[7]

Future Hall-of-Famer Hank Greenberg, born in 1911, was barely aware that baseball existed on the streets of Greenwich Village, New York, but when his family moved to the Bronx in the 1920s, Greenberg became an ardent Giants fan. Growing up to be a strong and strapping 6-foot-4-inch young man, the future home-run great began playing baseball for a local team, the Bay Parkways. When scouts from the Giants and Yankees spotted Greenberg's power hitting at .454, he was hired for a stint on the semipro circuit.

"My mother would say to me," Greenberg later recounted, "'Why are you wasting your time playing baseball? It's a bum's game.'"[8] Greenberg had been offered a college scholarship when major-league teams eagerly began bidding for his services. Reluctant to hurt his parents, Greenberg told the highest bidder that he would have to go to college first. But after the Detroit Tigers offered him $3,000 as a binder in case he changed his mind after his freshman year at college, Greenberg went to Tampa for spring training in 1929 and never resumed his education.

Greenberg was an exception. Very few Jewish men made it onto major-league teams. One, Andy Cohen, entered the major leagues in 1926 and played 226 games as an infielder with the New York Giants. Cohen had played on a minor-league team in Minneapolis and was subjected to considerable abuse. In Louisville, Kentucky, he later recounted:

> *A guy in the stands, a big guy ... kept hollering at me the whole game, "Christ killer." He hollered, "Christ killer this" and "Christ killer that." I got sick of it. I took a bat and went to the stands and looked up at him and said, "Yeah, come down here and I'll kill you, too."*[9]

In the Bronx, with Jewish fans plentiful in the bleachers, no one dared insult Cohen.

In other parts of the country, several players with common Jewish names like Cohen (or Cohn) changed them to names like Ewing, Cooney, Kane, and Bohne in order to have a better shot at the major leagues. But most baseball owners caught on and kept them out.

Throughout those years, organized baseball was a mirror reflection of society's racism and anti-Semitism. A powerful eugenics movement, later a model for Hitler's advisers, claimed to "prove" white supremacy. Mainstream magazines proclaimed Latinos to be "inferior" and a "eugenic menace." A best-selling book labeled Mexicans, perhaps because of their revolution in the 1910s, "born communists."[10]

Foster's Negro National League, centered in the Midwest, included a team called the Cuban Stars, which was made up mostly of Cuban players. An Eastern Colored League soon followed in 1923, and the Negro leagues conducted an annual World Series. The Negro leagues set up minor leagues in the South that spawned superstars like Satchel Paige. A group of African-American all-star players, including Cubans, traveled to Japan in 1927, seven years before Babe Ruth and Lou Gehrig arrived. Today, baseball is Japan's most popular sport.

In 1929 the stock market crashed. A devastating ten-year economic crisis known as the Great Depression began. Even the new middle class found itself plunged into poverty. Worst off were the nation's African Americans, Latinos, and Native Americans. Already at the bottom of the ladder, they were soon searching for simple survival.

Baseball had prospered in the 1920s, but by the early 1930s, for many people the fifty cents for a bleacher seat meant giving up a meal. As attendance dropped precipitously, owners undertook several measures to help keep the game alive. Not a single owner, however, proposed increasing the attendance of black and Latino fans by hiring dark-skinned stars for major-league teams.[11]

One measure taken by the owners of white baseball in 1933 was to hold the first major-league All-Star Game. That same year, black and Latino players initiated the Negro League East-West Game. Unlike white baseball, black and Latino baseball allowed the fans to choose by ballot who would play in the all-star matchup. Their East-West Game lasted until 1950.

Many of the Negro-league teams, never well financed, collapsed during the Great Depression. New ones rose from their ashes, though. They were funded in great part by one of the few businesses that could thrive during the depression —the illegal numbers racket. Alessandro "Alex" Pompez, a Cuban American born in Florida, owned the New York Cubans of the Negro National League. He helped Jewish-American gangster Dutch Schultz operate the numbers business in Harlem. Today, a legal version of the numbers game is called the lottery and is used by many states as a way of raising money for their sagging budgets.

The outstanding and incredibly popular play of Negro-league baseball greats—such as Paige, Josh Gibson, and Cuba's Martín Dihigo—in the 1920s and 1930s helped blaze the way to baseball's eventual racial integration. Gibson, who hit balls farther than Babe Ruth, blasted 75 home runs in 1931. Had racial privileges been reversed, Babe Ruth would have gone down in history as the "White Josh Gibson."[12] Dihigo, known for his playing all nine positions, tied Gibson for the Negro League home-run title in 1935 and won it in 1936.

Dihigo was the only Latino from the Negro-league era to be elected to the Hall of Fame in Cooperstown, New York, as well as to the Halls of Fame in Cuba, Mexico, and Venezuela. Standing 6 feet 3 inches tall and weighing 225 pounds, the powerful Cuban was arguably the best ballplayer of all time. People nicknamed him "the Team Man." Dihigo compiled a lifetime batting average of .304 and, as a pitcher, won 256 games while losing only 133. He frequently won his league's batting and pitching titles *in the same season*!

In a famous 1926 pitching duel at Almendares Park near Havana, Dihigo bested the lighter-skinned major leaguer Dolf Luque, 1-0. Luque often stated that his fellow Cubans José Méndez and Dihigo would have become even more famous than he if Jim Crow had not excluded them from the majors. At age forty, Méndez had won the deciding game of the 1924 Negro League World Series by throwing a shutout for Kansas City.

In 1937 Rafael Trujillo, the U.S.-backed dictator of the Dominican Republic, was upset that his Ciudad Trujillo [Santo Domingo] team in the Dominican professional baseball league had lost to a team from the rural outpost of San Pedro de Macorís. He contacted the great pitcher of Gus Greenlee's Pittsburgh Crawfords, Satchel Paige, to bring some African-American players to Ciudad Trujillo to ensure the team of a league title.

Guaranteeing good pay, the dictator assembled one of baseball's all-time greatest teams, with players like Cool Papa Bell, Dihigo, Josh Gibson, and Paige. After one of their rare losses of a game, the men were terrified by the appearance of the tyrant's gun-toting militia, who shot into the air and informed them "El Presidente doesn't lose."[13] Trujillo's team won the Dominican title and returned to the United States to sweep the *Denver Post* semipro tournament as the Ciudad Trujillo All-Stars.

The Negro-league players saw little hope for an end to Jim Crow in baseball. But already there were the beginnings of a civil rights struggle that would win, too late for most of them. Multiracial coalitions took shape to combat

Although Hall-of-Famer Martín Dihigo spent much of his career in Latin America, he played several seasons with the New York Cubans of the Negro National League. The Cuban great played all positions and was a great hitter.

mass unemployment and end Jim Crow. By the mid-1930s, unemployed blacks and Latinos outnumbered jobless whites three to one. Coalitions of blacks, Latinos, and whites, many of them Jewish Americans, fought and won a trickle of government aid for the millions of unemployed. A powerful labor movement was born.

The Ciudad Trujillo team poses for a photo. In 1937, dictator Rafael Trujillo brought several of the top Negro-league players to the Dominican Republic to ensure that his team would win the country's professional-league title.

With anti-democratic Nazi and fascist governments taking power in Europe, it was embarrassing for U.S. government leaders and journalists to speak out against the white supremacist Nazis when racism in all its ugly forms was so obvious in the United States. A few white sports columnists and newsmen began hammering away at the issue of Jim Crow in baseball.

In 1935 the voice of one of the most prominent radio newscasters, Westbrook Pegler, was heard on radios all over the nation speaking about the "silly unwritten law that bars dark Babe Ruths and [Dizzie] Deans from the fame and money they deserve." Dan Parker of the *New York Daily News* wrote that "there is no good reason why in a country that calls itself a Democracy, intolerance should exist on the sportsfield, that most democratic of all meeting places."[14]

As Adolf Hitler put forward Germany's greatest athletes as proof of "Aryan supremacy," African Americans cheered when track-and-field star Jesse Owens walked away with gold and silver medals at the 1936 Olympics held in Berlin right under Hitler's nose. Two years later, African-American boxer Joe Louis, "the Brown Bomber," knocked out Max Schmelling, Hitler's prized boxing champion.

But there was also a dark side to the response to Nazism. As Hitler's super-racist philosophy took hold in Germany and then swept over Europe, the milder virus of racism and anti-Semitism that had lived a long and healthy life in the United States gave way to a far more virulent strain that jumped the ocean and spread over the land of the free.

In Germany, by 1938, official anti-Semitic laws made life for Jews impossible. No Jewish families dreamed in their wildest imaginings that death camps would be their final fate, but many saw sufficient danger signs to attempt to leave their homeland. The U.S. Congress voted down legislation aimed at lifting the harsh immigration quotas of 1924 and permitting endangered refugees a chance to enter the country. Many of the people turned away by U.S. immigration officials later died in the gas chambers of Nazi concentration camps.

By 1939, when it was obvious that U.S. participation in the war was inevitable, powerful hate groups loudly blamed Jewish Americans not only for the Great Depression but for the war itself. In many cities thousands of pro-Nazis of the German American Bund held regular parades, bedecked in uniforms decorated with Nazi swastikas. In 1942, with World War II raging, a Roper poll announced its findings that the majority of Americans considered Jewish Americans a threat, second only to Japanese Americans, who were already being herded off into detention camps for the duration of the war.

Several African Americans and Latinos spoke out against these outrages, but they had little power to change government policy. Furthermore, their own struggles for justice were heating up again. In the late 1930s, as defense plants opened and recruitment to the armed services was hastily stepped up, they believed that the moment was ripe to increase pressure for job equality.

Hank Greenberg's first full year in the majors had been 1933, the year Hitler came to power. Despite the increased anti-Semitism, Greenberg had twice been named Most Valuable Player. No one dared ignore his astonishing home-run record as the Detroit Tigers won the pennant in 1934, 1935, 1940, and 1945. In 1935, Greenberg's Jewish origins had become the focus of attention when he refused to play on the high Jewish holiday, Yom Kippur, even though his team was in the middle of a hot pennant race.

It was customary for players on the bench to taunt opposition players when they came up to bat. This "bench jockeying" became racist when Jews or Latinos stepped to the plate. In the 1935 World Series, the Chicago Cubs "crucified Hank Greenberg for being a Jew and taunted Jewish umpire Dolly Stark as a Christ killer."[15] The plate umpire had to stop the game to warn the anti-Semitic bench jockeys to shut up or be expelled from the game.[16] But anti-Semitism proved more painful in 1938. Greenberg had hit 58 home runs by the last week of the season and with only 2 more he would tie Babe Ruth's record. Another famous Jewish ballplayer, Al Rosen, later commented how anti-Semitism was unleashed against letting a Jew break the Babe's record. Greenberg never saw a good pitch in the season's final games.

But no matter how strongly anti-Semitism touched every aspect of American life, Jewish men *did* play major-league baseball and dark-skinned Latinos and African Americans *did not*. Usually the color line remained an unmentioned reality, but on July 29, 1938, this changed. During a radio interview before a Yankee–White Sox game, Yankee outfielder Jake Powell was asked how he kept in shape during the off-season. Millions of baseball fans, waiting for the game to begin, couldn't believe what they heard!

Powell told his interviewer that he worked as a police-man in Dayton, Ohio, "where he kept in shape by crack-ing niggers over the head."[17] The radio went dead for a moment and then the announcer returned to apologize. The Yankees quickly ordered a ten-day suspension for Powell, but from all over the nation demands rolled in that Powell be banned from baseball. Petitions flooded Yankee headquarters. Bottles were thrown at Powell in Washington, D.C. Every sports columnist felt obligated to comment on the incident. Some even raised the larger issue of baseball integration. Powell apologized but it had little impact. Behind the scenes the Yankees tried to trade him. There were no takers. In 1940, after injuries kept him on the bench, Powell left the major leagues.

But Powell was not alone in his thinking; he was sim-ply noisier about it. One third of major-league players had been raised in the South and quite a few backed the Ku Klux Klan. On the other hand, although a few stars like Rogers Hornsby and Al Simmons would not work with barnstorming teams that played games against Negro-league teams, most players joined in the interracial competitions. Dizzy Dean, who had enjoyed pitching duels with the great Satchel Paige, said, "It's too bad those colored boys don't play in the big leagues, because they sure got some great players."[18] Powell's racist remarks brought the color-line question out of the closet. Westbrook Pegler accused the national pastime of dealing with "Negroes as Adolf Hitler treats the Jews."[19]

By the spring of 1940 it was clear that no negotiations would deter Adolf Hitler from his plan to rule the world. Nazi troops goose-stepped across Europe. German planes rained bombs on London. Hitler's tanks rolled toward Moscow. Unarmed Russian Jewish men, women, and chil-dren were lined up in front of trenches and brutally exe-cuted. It was the opening salvo of the Holocaust, Hitler's plan to wipe out the Jewish population of Europe.

As London's hospitals filled with bomb victims, the

American Red Cross organized a Blood for Britain program. Dr. Charles Drew, an African-American scientist who had discovered a method to preserve blood for transfusions by using blood plasma as a substitute for whole blood, was named to head up the program. Shortly after he accepted the post, Dr. Drew was ordered to separate the plasma vials *according to race.* He resigned at a much publicized press conference.

African Americans, Latinos, and antiracist white Americans were incensed, but the incident that led to Dr. Drew's resignation was only a tiny part of their anger. As thousands of jobs opened in defense plants, it became clear that few blacks and Latinos would be hired. A powerful Latino civil rights group, the Spanish-Speaking People's Congress, linked arms with the NAACP and the Jewish People's Committee to launch the Council for the Protection of Minority Rights. Black anger ratcheted up another notch when the War Department refused to integrate the military.

Prominent African-American leaders, including union organizer A. Philip Randolph, announced plans for a March on Washington on July 1, 1940, to protest those inequities. As support for the demonstration swelled, President Roosevelt issued an executive order that ignored the question of military integration but established the Fair Employment Practices Committee (FEPC) to enforce fair hiring in factories with government contracts. Black leaders accepted the compromise, and the march was canceled.

As Nazi propaganda loudly announced the superiority of the "Aryan" race, African-American volunteers were turned down by the military. The carefully limited number of black draftees found themselves assigned to special departments, such as Engineers Corps or Quartermaster Corps, where they were relegated to cleanup, delivery, cooking, and other "service duties." In the defense plants, so-called "arsenals of democracy," the FEPC, with little real power, did little about the fact that most black and Latino

Armed with clubs, pipes, and bottles, a mob of U.S. sailors swagger through the streets of Los Angeles during the 1943 zoot suit riots. During the disturbance, drunken sailors attacked Latinos, African-Americans, and Asians.

job seekers were turned away. Dismayed African-American leaders called for a war on two fronts. The V-for-victory symbol became a Double V for blacks: victory in the war and victory at home against racism.

On December 7, 1941, Japan bombed Pearl Harbor. Within hours the United States was at war with Germany, Italy, and Japan. The war did not go well for the Allies at first. But although replacements were sorely needed to take the place of the dead and wounded, black soldiers were not allowed to fight. Most of them remained at army bases, carrying out menial service assignments. Latinos, on the other hand, were given combat duty and went on to earn more Medals of Honor than any other group.

Some married white men complained that their draft boards ordered them into service but allowed single black men to stay home. The truth was that Army officials were hard pressed to maintain segregation and yet continue to draft African Americans. Most Army training camps were located in southern states where Jim Crow laws made it mandatory to separate black and white soldiers in public places. Black soldiers typically preferred to remain on base rather than risk being attacked by white bigots in nearby cities and towns. When they did venture off base, they often passed restaurants where they were not welcome. Looking in, they would see white soldiers inside dining and fraternizing with German prisoners of war.

At home, many people had hoped that the fight against the most infamous racists on the face of the earth would eventually improve conditions for minorities in the United States. Instead, the situation seemed to grow worse. During the 1943 "zoot suit" riots in California, U.S. sailors on a drunken rampage viciously attacked Latinos, blacks, and Asians with the approval of some of their commanding officers. Skin color was as usual the unspoken criterion for these abominations. German Americans were typically left in peace.[20]

When African-American and Latino workers were finally hired or occasionally promoted in the defense plants, some white workers turned to violence. The worst racial riot took place in Detroit in 1943, when federal troops were called in to restore order. Radio Tokyo gleefully described the incident and mocked American "democracy," which continued to "deny the Negroes the opportunity to engage in respectable jobs ... and periodically will run amuck to lynch Negroes individually or to slaughter them whole-sale."[21]

Under these conditions, the nascent struggle to integrate baseball developed into a full-blown movement.

4
cuatro

JIM CROW

MUST GO!

I cannot stand and sing the anthem. I cannot salute the flag. I know that I am a black man in a white world. In 1972, in 1947, at my birth in 1919, I know that I never had it made.
— Jackie Robinson, from the
Introduction to *I Never Had It Made*[1]

For many years, few baseball people spoke about it. But they all knew the ugly truth: there was only one thing keeping African Americans and dark-skinned Latinos out of organized baseball—skin color.

The Brooklyn Dodgers' manager Leo Durocher, excited by the talents of Cuban shortstop Silvio García, let it slip. "Where the hell have you been hiding?..." he was overheard telling García. "If we could just do a little something about that skin color...." Leo "the Lip" Durocher, not known for his ability to keep quiet, said he "would hire colored players if they were not barred by the owners. I've seen a million good ones."[2]

National League president Ford Frick was reported as telling several players, "If only you were white." He also tried to cover for baseball's racism by inaccurately stating: "Colored people did not have a chance to play during slavery, and so were late in developing proficiency."[3] *Washington Post* columnist Shirley Povich stated bluntly that "Only one thing is keeping [Latinos and African Americans] out of the big leagues—the color of their skin."[4] One day, fans at Chicago's Wrigley Field saw large letters scrawled on the wall: "Does Hitler bar Negro ballplayers?"[5] Civil rights coalitions stepped up their call for an end to Jim Crow.

Before long, some major-league team owners, hurting financially, were being told about the potential advantages of integration. Receipts had dwindled during the Great Depression. Then, as major-league players were drafted or volunteered to serve in the military to fight World War II, their teams' ranks were depleted. Team owners thought it unwise to ask for draft exemptions for ballplayers, yet President Roosevelt asked them to keep the game going for the country's morale. Many Negro-league players were too old to be drafted into the military, and others were not called up, probably because of racism, so they were available to fill depleted team rosters.

For the first time after the jobless years of the Great Depression, African Americans had a few dollars to pay admission to ball games, and they packed the stands at Negro-league games. Baseball executives could not avoid the dollar-and-cents reality. At a night game in Washington, D.C., 29,000 fans came out to cheer as Satchel Paige pitched against the Homestead Grays. An afternoon game in the same stadium on the same day between the Washington Senators and Boston Red Sox drew a crowd of under 5,000.

As World War II dragged on, baseball's manpower shortage went from bad to worse. Less than half of the major-league players in 1941 were still playing in 1944. Big drawing cards, including Joe DiMaggio, Ted Williams, and Hank Greenberg, had gone off to fight. In desperation, the St. Louis Browns hired one-armed outfielder Pete Grey. A talented white junior high school student was brought into the majors. Fears grew that professional baseball might have to close down for the duration of the war. It became more and more necessary for club owners to look over the gold mine of talented black and Latino players in the Negro leagues.

But the owners continued to follow their own racist views, or at least to bow to the racist sentiments of mainstream America.

Unwilling to hire African Americans, some began imitating the Senators' Clark Griffith. Almost fifty Cuban players signed U.S. baseball contracts during the war. Most, but not all, of them signed with Washington and its farm teams. Some Mexicans and Puerto Ricans were also admitted to the big leagues, although, like the Cubans, they were promptly released or sent back to the minors at war's end.

The world championship series in amateur baseball (not to be confused with the World Series, the fall classic played in the United States)—which had started in England in 1938, when only the United States showed up—was becoming popular in Latin America and drawing the attention of a lot of U.S. baseball scouts. Throughout the 1940s, when Cuba hosted five consecutive championship series,

Five members of the Havana Cubans, including catcher Miguel González (center), pose before a game. The Havana Cubans played its first season in the Florida State League in 1946.

the "Mundiales," as they became known, drew teams from around the world to compete on an equal footing without regard to race —quite a contrast to U.S. baseball. More than half the time, through 1972, Cuba's team won the Mundiales.

Griffith joined Cuban promoter Roberto Maduro to create the Havana Cubans minor-league team in 1946. Playing its home games in the newly built Gran Stadium, the Havana Cubans dominated the Florida State League and produced such future major-league stars as Camilo Pascual, Julio Becquer, and Sandy Consuegra.

Back in the United States, the Citizen's Committee to End Jim Crow in baseball regularly picketed Yankee Stadium, carrying signs with slogans like "If we are able to stop bullets, why not balls?"[6] A delegation from several

CIO labor unions visited Commissioner Landis, urging him to act. In New York State in 1942, the Quinn-Ives Act banned job discrimination. Farther south in St. Louis, the Cardinals and Browns desegregated Sportsman's Park.

The most persistent sports columnists—such as Sam Lacy of the *Chicago Defender*, Joe Bostic of the African-American newspaper *People's Voice*, and Nat Lowe of the

Communist Party newspaper *Daily Worker*—continued in vain to push the owners to sign up black and Latino players. "No Room at the Yankee Inn" was the title of Bostic's Christmas-season column in 1943.

Still, no dark-skinned players appeared in the majors.

Other voices in the baseball press openly opposed racial integration. A headline in *Sporting News* on August 6, 1942, proclaimed "NO GOOD FROM RAISING RACE ISSUE." The article insisted that only "agitators" favored "race mixing."[7]

During spring training for the 1943 season another tactic was tried. In California, Jackie Roosevelt Robinson, an all-American UCLA football star, showed up at the Chicago White Sox training ground in Pasadena with Negro league pitcher Nate Moreland. They asked for a tryout. White Sox manager Jimmy Dykes agreed and later said of Robinson, "He's worth $50,000 of anybody's money." Nevertheless, the two men heard nothing further from the team. Moreland's bitter comment was, "I can play in Mexico, but I have to fight for America where I can't play."[8]

Negro-league team owners proposed the formation of a major-league black team. Pittsburgh Pirate owner William Benswanger, urged by the *Pittsburgh Courier* to break the color line, agreed to some tryouts and then dodged the issue. Leo Durocher declared that he would hire black players if he were permitted to. There was no way that Commissioner Landis could avoid responding. He declared that

> *There is no rule, formal or informal, or any understanding—unwritten, subterranean, or sub-anything—against the hiring of Negro players by the teams of organized ball. If Durocher wants to sign one, or 25 Negro players it is alright.*[9]

Actually, throughout his long tenure in office, Landis had steadfastly prohibited any discussion of dropping the color line.

National League president Ford Frick also now publicly declared that he would "welcome a Negro player in the National League."[10] Black leaders were permitted to speak before a major-league owners meeting in 1943. But after they left the room, there was no further discussion.

Bill Veeck, the twenty-nine-year-old son of ex–Chicago Cubs owner William Veeck, Sr., decided to call the bluffs of Landis and Frick. Veeck, who had bought a minor-league team in Milwaukee in 1941, was a popular figure with players. Hank Greenberg wrote that Veeck was the "only owner I ever knew who gave a damn about his players."[11] In 1943, Veeck almost succeeded in integrating baseball on a grand scale.

Veeck was in the final hours of closing a deal to buy the Philadelphia Phillies. He planned to strengthen the Phillies by signing up several top-flight black players. He traveled to Chicago to inform Commissioner Landis of his decision. The two had a friendly meeting. But when Veeck returned to Philadelphia the next day he learned that National League president Frick had blocked the deal and arranged for the sale of the Phillies to a wealthy lumber dealer named William Cox. The following year Cox was banished from baseball for betting on the games.

Even though the club owners refused to improve their teams by dropping the color line, something had to be done to bring in the dollars. Philip K. Wrigley, owner of the Chicago Cubs, organized the All-American Girls Professional Baseball League, composed of four teams that played in major-league ballparks. Women had played baseball for decades, the games almost always taking place in secluded areas of women's colleges. In the 1880s several barnstorming women's teams had played softball on the road, attracting audiences by creating an almost circuslike atmosphere. The Amateur Softball Association was organized in the early 1930s, and by 1943, 40,000 women's softball teams were part of it, playing night games near defense plants, where some of the players worked the day shift.

But the new women's league played hardball and kept up a grueling 108-game schedule, drawing 176,000 fans to games between teams with names like Barney Ross's

Adorables and Balian Ice Cream Beauties. Members of the league attended charm school to learn hairdo and make-up tips and were not permitted to wear T-shirts, pants, and other "masculine" attire that made it easier to pitch and run bases. Even after the war in 1948, the by-then ten teams of the league drew close to a million fans. After the advent of televised baseball in the 1950s, the league finally folded in 1954. This neglected episode in baseball history was recalled in the popular 1992 film *A League of Their Own*.

Five hundred women had played professional baseball for more than ten years. All of them had been white. Just as female factory workers who had kept production going during the war were dismissed afterwards, so women were asked to play baseball but afterwards they were told to stay out of "a man's world." Females were not even allowed to play Little League baseball until 1974, after several legal battles.

Commissioner Landis died after the close of the 1944 season, and Senator Albert "Happy" Chandler became baseball commissioner. Hopes for the integration of baseball soared when Rick Roberts, sportswriter for the *Pittsburgh Courier*, interviewed Chandler and asked him about using black players. Chandler told Roberts, "If they can fight and die in Okinawa, Guadalcanal, in the South Pacific, they can play baseball in America. When I give my word you can count on it."[12] Years later, Chandler claimed the credit for having integrated baseball. Yet in 1948 he supported the Dixiecrat segregationist candidate in the presidential contest and in 1968 aspired to become the running mate of diehard segregationist George Wallace. Chandler had the power to approve or veto all baseball contracts, but not one contract appeared for a dark-skinned player.

In the last years of the war, baseball remained lily white, and civil rights coalition activists had more-important issues on their agenda. By 1944, the war had turned in favor of the Allies. Black soldiers, still denied combat duty, were demanding a role in the final defeat of the Axis powers. On June 6, 1944, D-Day, the United States landed an all-white invasion force on the coast of France. After a storm of protest, a few African-American units were sent into action in the closing months of the war and served heroically, although few Americans ever heard about their exploits.[13] They did, however, hear the full details of the horrors inside the Nazi concentration camps throughout Europe. More people than ever before were determined to make American democracy a reality for everyone.

Some club owners had long claimed that they could not be accused of discrimination since no dark-skinned players ever showed up at tryouts. When the first postwar Dodgers spring training camp opened in Bear Mountain, New York, in April 1945, African-American sports columnist Joe Bostic appeared with two Negro-league players.

"Rickey went berserk almost," Bostic later recalled. The Dodgers owner called it a publicity stunt and told Bostic, "You are defeating your own aims."[14] The tryout took place, but the players received no further word. By opening day at Yankee Stadium in 1945, all-white teams were once more scheduled to play and the usual civil rights picketers appeared.

New York was not the only city where baseball teams were under pressure to integrate. In Boston, the Red Sox and Braves came under fire as well. Isadore Muchnick, a Jewish city council member elected by a heavily African-American district, pressured ball-club owners to invite non-white players for serious tryouts. Red Sox general manager Eddie Collins told him indignantly, "We have never had a single request for a tryout by a colored applicant. It is beyond my understanding how anyone can insinuate or believe that all ballplayers, regardless of race, color or creed, have not been treated in the American way as far as having an equal opportunity to play for the Red Sox."[15]

In mid-April 1945, Wendell Smith, an African-American reporter, appeared at Boston's Fenway Park with Jackie Robinson, recently hired by the Kansas City Monarchs; Sam Jethroe, leading Negro-league hitter in 1944; and Philadelphia Stars second baseman Marvin

Williams, also a heavy hitter. Left cooling their heels for two days, the trio finally received halfhearted tryouts after *Boston Daily Record* sportswriter Dave Egan commented that Fenway Park was "in the city of Boston, Massachusetts, and not in the city of Mobile, Alabama." During the tryouts, Red Sox players and manager Joe Cronin were nowhere to be seen. Cronin later admitted, "We just accepted things the way they were."[16]

Apparently these efforts and the publicity surrounding them had an impact. About a month after the Dodgers tryouts, Branch Rickey called a press conference. Calling Bostic's effort Communist-inspired and bad-mouthing the Negro leagues, he announced the formation of the United States League (USL) for black ballplayers. Some interpreted Rickey's move as an effort to circumvent the need to purchase talent from the Negro leagues. Others saw the whole plan as a hoax, a way to stave off efforts to enforce New York's Quinn-Ives antidiscrimination act. Rickey's new league eventually folded. Effa Manley, owner of the Negro league's Newark Eagles, noted that Rickey could not drum up "suitable playing sites and vital fan support on a widespread scale."[17]

Meanwhile, other events began to have an impact on baseball. Reports of violent attacks on African Americans escalated. In South Carolina, when black army veteran Isaac Woodard, Jr., rode on a bus toward home in February 1946, police dragged him from the bus, beat him into unconsciousness, and permanently blinded him. With President Harry Truman making speeches on restoring freedom and democracy to all of the nations of the world, 13 million black Americans insisted on voting rights, full equality, and an end to violence and lynching. Latinos added their voices to the call.

The nascent civil rights alliance between African Americans, Latinos, and Jewish Americans expanded, taking in Japanese Americans, heartsick from their incarceration during the war, and other concerned citizens. Hundreds of conferences were held across the nation, with participants calling for racial and religious tolerance. Court cases were initiated against segregation in schools and other public places. When Mexican Americans in California sued against school segregation, supporting testimony (amicus curiae briefs) was filed by several organizations, including the NAACP and the American Jewish Congress.[18]

Forty different human rights and civil rights organizations put together the National Emergency Committee Against Mob Violence, urging President Truman to act to ensure civil rights. When hearing from this group about the blinding of Isaac Woodard, Truman exclaimed: "My God! I had no idea that it was as terrible as that! We've got to do something!"[19]

The president and his advisers had other worries too. They feared that with the closing down of war industries, the nation's economy would plummet back to the economic disaster days of the Great Depression. But if armaments factories were to continue, there had to be a reason, a new enemy. That enemy turned out to be Communism.

Throughout the world, especially in Asia and Africa, people who had lived under the yoke of colonialism were fighting for their independence. In creating their new economies, they typically chose between two economic systems: the socialist model of the Soviet Union or the capitalist model of the United States. Because most of the colonial peoples of the world were not white, the racism prevalent in the United States influenced many countries to opt for a socialist system. Racism became a U.S. Achilles' heel in the new Cold War between the United States and its former wartime ally, the Soviet Union.[20]

Opponents of Truman's new Cold War policies were labeled "un-American." Supporters of segregation learned quickly that they could undermine the efforts of the expanding civil rights alliance by calling its supporters "Communists." But red-baiting alone was a weak response to the relentless Soviet campaign to highlight what was, after all, a shocking reality—racism in the United States.

President Truman ordered the creation of the

President's Committee on Civil Rights (PCCR) to look into ways for protecting people's civil rights. The PCCR report recommended Congress pass legislation for a panoply of civil rights. America's minorities were disheartened. Congress, after all, had not even been willing to keep the weak wartime FEPC afloat. There were two demands, however, that did not require congressional action. One was military integration, attainable by an executive order by the commander in chief, Truman—a step not taken until 1948 and not fully implemented until 1950. The other was baseball integration. All it would take would be one baseball team owner who hired any of the countless talented players from the Negro leagues or Latin America's leagues.

Realizing that the other baseball club owners, fans, and players would be more willing to accept Latin Americans with lighter-brown complexions than African Americans, Dodgers owner Rickey, acting in secret, told his scouts to scour Latin America for players for his new "Brown Dodgers" team that would play in Ebbets Field when the Dodgers were out of town. The scouts brought to Rickey the Cuban pitcher Silvio García, whose talents had so excited Leo Durocher.

García did not meet Rickey's behavioral standards. Rickey wanted the first dark-skinned major leaguer to be someone who could take the expected insults and remain silent. But when he interviewed García and asked him, "What would you do if a white American slapped your face?" the proud Cuban responded, "I kill him."[21]

Rickey looked for a man who would have impeccable credentials, someone educated, controlled, beyond reproach, someone who could head off incidents by playing deaf and dumb. He decided to interview Jackie Robinson, who had a long history at UCLA playing on the integrated football team and had played a season at shortstop for the Kansas City Monarchs of the Negro National League. Apparently, Rickey did not realize how much of a fighter Jackie Robinson was. In 1944, while serving in the U.S. Army, Jackie had refused to sit in the back of a bus at Fort Hood,

Texas, and faced a court-martial. Acquitted, he had been honorably discharged in late 1944.

Thirteen days after the end of the war, on August 28, 1945, Jackie Robinson entered Rickey's office. Rickey held the plum out—a contract with the Montreal Royals of the International League, a Dodgers all-white farm team. Then Rickey launched into a dramatic enactment of what Robinson could expect, shouting out vicious racial insults. Not only that, Rickey told Robinson, but there could be deliberate beanballs and spikings as well. "His acting was so convincing that I found myself chain-gripping my fingers behind my back," Robinson later remembered.[22]

Robinson assured Rickey that he could control himself and accepted the offer of a bonus of $3,500 and a contract for $600 a month. There were no promises of future promotion to the Dodgers. For several weeks there were rumors of the signing but no official announcement.

Robinson told the good news to his family and his teammate Roy Campanella. Campanella was upset. Rickey had offered Campanella a low-paying contract with the Brooklyn Brown Dodgers, and Campanella, perhaps out of loyalty to the Negro leagues, had turned him down. Now he was worried that he had forfeited a chance to play with the Dodgers Montreal farm team and a shot at the Dodgers.

On October 23, 1945, the Dodgers' decision was made public at a press conference in Montreal. Branch Rickey was not on hand. The news brought a wide variety of reactions. Joe Bostic hoped it wasn't merely a trick. Dodger outfielder Dixie Walker, a native Alabaman, remarked, "As long as he isn't with the Dodgers, I'm not worried." Rogers Hornsby said flatly, "It won't work out. A mixed baseball team differs from other sports because ballplayers on the road live much closer together."[23]

Newsmen reported that Negro-league players like Satchel Paige had mixed feelings, happy about the chance of baseball's integration but hurt that they had not been chosen. Hall-of-Famer Buck Leonard later recalled, "We had a whole lot better ballplayers than Jackie, but Jackie was chosen [by Rickey] 'cause he had played football with white boys."[24] Other Kansas City players remembered Robinson for his short temper whenever he was faced with segregation during the 1945 barnstorming season, not exactly the image of the patient saint Rickey was seeking.

Right up to the present, baseball writers have debated the reasons for Branch Rickey's decision and his choice of Jackie Robinson for his "experiment." Rickey himself provided several reasons for his decision, few of them credible.[25]

Bill Veeck and others presented a strong argument that Robinson's signing was based on financial need. Renting out stadiums in the off-season was an important source of income. The Yankees and Giants both rented their fields to teams from the Negro leagues, but when the Brooklyn Eagles moved to Newark, New Jersey, in 1934, the Dodgers lost about $100,000 every year. Veeck believed that Rickey knew that whether or not Robinson ever was promoted to the Dodgers, black baseball fans would become Dodgers fans when Robinson integrated the Montreal Royals. Veeck wrote:

> Rickey wanted money. The Yankees and the Giants split [the Negro- league money] and Rickey wanted a third of it. The Yankees and Giants would not give him a third. And that is how he signed Jackie Robinson.[26]

It seems likely that the success of the Negro-leagues' East-West game in drawing big crowds contributed to the major leagues' finally integrating baseball. As Negro-league third baseman "Gentleman" Dave Malarcher put it:

> When the Major Leagues saw 50,000 to 60,000 fans in that ballpark—well Rickey saw he had something more than a little black boy.... He saw what black fans would do for the pocketbook of the Major Leagues.[27]

Barnstorming games played by white teams against black teams had long been a big moneymaker. The year Rickey signed Robinson, batting star Stan Musial of the

St. Louis Cardinals "complained that his share of the World Series money came to less than half of the $10,000 paycheck he made from one interracial barnstorming tour."[28]

Although Rickey certainly knew about the pickets marching around the stadiums shouting "Jim Crow Must Go," he always insisted that the protest movement had no influence on his decision. Every Sunday New York City mayor Fiorella La Guardia went on radio, reading comic strips for children and discussing the political controversies of the week. Feeling the pressure of the anti–Jim Crow protestors, on one of his shows Mayor La Guardia talked about the work of his newly appointed Mayor's Commission on Baseball. Hearing that La Guardia planned to announce that baseball would soon be signing Negro players, Rickey asked him to postpone his announcement so that no one would think such a decision had been forced on him. La Guardia complied, and a little later Jackie Robinson was signed to play with the Montreal team.

Once again Latinos played a key role in U.S. baseball's integration. With spring training several months off, Robinson played winter baseball in Venezuela as a member of the all-black and Latino United States All-Stars. The Venezuelans, many of them of African or mixed descent, loved it.

Campanella wrote Rickey from Venezuela, expressing his interest in becoming part of the experiment. On March 1, 1946, Campanella received a cable inviting him to meet with Rickey right away. Not long after their meeting, Rickey announced that Robinson would not integrate baseball alone. Campanella and Don Newcombe would work together as catcher and pitcher at a lower level of the Dodger farm system and then move up to Montreal. Black pitchers John Wright and Roy Partlow would also be assigned a spot in the Dodgers farm system.

In January 1946 Robinson returned to California and married his college sweetheart, Rachel Isum. Then the two of them packed their bags and left for spring training at the Brooklyn Dodgers training camp in Daytona Beach, Florida.

Rachel, a native Californian, was horrified by the South's severe segregation practices. She and Jackie found "special" inferior accommodations waiting for them at Daytona Beach. Because of the racial tensions in the South, Campanella and Newcombe were told not to report for spring training.

Even in the North, farm-team managers were not ecstatic over baseball integration. Remembering back, Don Newcombe said, "What kind of animals were we that nobody wanted us?"[29] There was one exception: Buzzie Bavasi, the young general manager at Nashua, New Hampshire, who said he cared only about playing ability.

Rickey never paid a penny for Robinson's or other Negro-league players' contracts. Newark Eagles owner Effa Manley noted that he "didn't even say thank you." But black owners couldn't protest too much. "The Negro fans would never have forgiven us for keeping a Negro out of the major leagues," said one.[30]

Before the 1946 season opened, Rickey quietly sent African-American player John Wright to join Robinson on the Montreal Royals. A few days before opening day, a *Chicago Defender* editorial commented, "It is ironical that America, supposedly the cradle of democracy, is forced to send the first two Negroes in baseball to Canada in order for them to be accepted."[31] And accepted they were. In Montreal there were few problems. On April 18, 1946, opening day, Robinson went 4 for 5 with 2 stolen bases as the Royals destroyed the Jersey City Giants 14-1.

At road games in Syracuse and Baltimore, white fans booed and taunted Robinson. Back in their room, Rachel Robinson wept. When the news spread of the mistreatment of the visiting Montreal team, 10,000 black fans showed up for a Sunday doubleheader in Baltimore to cheer as 15,000 whites booed.[32]

That year the Louisville, Kentucky, Colonels won the American Association title, making it necessary for the Montreal Royals, winners in the International League, to play the Little World Series championship in Louisville.

The Jim Crow section of Louisville's Parkway Field seated fewer than 500 people, scarcely enough of a cheering section to drown out the boos and curses from the white-only section. Montreal won 8-5, winning the Little World Series. Back in Montreal Robinson was given a hero's welcome. From Rickey's vantage point, he had passed the test with flying colors, remaining cool under fire and helping to win a championship.

Realizing that Florida and the South were unreceptive of his "new look" teams, Rickey forked out the extra money and moved all his players to Havana, Cuba, for 1947's spring training. Rickey knew that Cuban fans, among the most ardent baseball aficionados in the world, would treat Robinson well.

Even in Cuba, though, all was not equal. The Dodgers stayed at the luxurious all-white Hotel Nacional, eating imported steaks, fruits, and vegetables. The white Montreal Royals were housed at a plush school, the Havana Military Academy, and also dined on imported food to avoid dysentery. Robinson, Partlow, and Newcombe were sent to a run-down hotel and given a food allowance to eat in local restaurants. Robinson developed stomach troubles, perhaps from the food but more likely from the continued insults to his dignity. He did not play very well and Cuban fans, who had seen far better Cuban players, soon turned their cheers into high-pitched whistles—Cuban-style boos.

After spring training, the Dodgers and Royals went on to Panama to play some exhibition games. Dark-skinned Panamanian fans looked forward to seeing Robinson. A dozen Panamanian baseball stars had played in the Negro leagues. The Dodgers' game against General Electric, the champions of the Panama Professional League, drew only 2,000 fans, but Robinson and the Montreal Royals–GE game drew 6,000. Robinson hit .519 in the 12 games played, as Panama's fans rose to their feet cheering.

Rumors circulated that at a secret meeting of major-league owners a report had been written urging the continued segregation of baseball. A vote to endorse the report had been 15-1, with only Rickey in opposition. After the vote, copies of the report were collected and destroyed. It was not until the 1980s that Happy Chandler, who had held on to his copy, made it public.

Looking back to those days, it may seem ridiculous that there was such an enormous fuss over rumors of *one* African-American ballplayer joining *one* major-league team. Sportswriters debated the issue week after week, some questioning Robinson's age (he was twenty-seven at the time) and his physical condition. Famed Cleveland fastballer Bob Feller flatly stated that there was *no* qualified black player, characterizing Robinson as a muscle-bound player with no future.[33]

Rickey hesitated to proceed. He held a secret meeting on February 5, 1947, with Brooklyn's African-American leaders, all of them professional men. He told them that *if* he brought Robinson on to the Dodger team, "The biggest threat to his success—is the Negro people themselves. You'll strut. You'll wear badges.... You'll get drunk. You'll fight. You'll be arrested. You'll wine and dine the player until he is fat and futile. You'll symbolize his importance into a national comedy... and an ultimate tragedy."[34] Claiming that black fans in Chicago had ruined Charlie "Chief Tokohama" Grant's career in 1901 with their overenthusiasm (see chapter 1), he urged the assembled men to do all they could to convince black fans not to cheer too wildly or arrive at ball games with liquor under their belts. When news of the meeting leaked out, black sportswriters lambasted the racial stereotyping. Joe Bostic later said, "I've never forgiven any of those guys for either attending or those who did attend for not showing their resentment and indignation at the effrontery."[35]

On April 10, 1947, Rickey told Robinson the news of his promotion to the Dodgers and announced the official decision to the press. New York newspapers hailed the news with relief. Rickey worried about the reaction of white fans and his southern-raised players. Some of Robinson's new teammates, led by Dixie Walker, petitioned Rickey to exclude him. Joining Walker were Hugh Casey, a pitcher from Georgia; Bobby Bragan, an outspoken catcher from Birmingham, Alabama; and two northerners, Carl Furillo and Eddie Stanky, both from Pennsylvania.

Dodgers manager Durocher and his actress wife, Laraine Day, took Kentucky-raised shortstop Pee Wee Reese and pitcher Kirby Higbe to dinner and asked them to help derail the petitioners. Robinson could help them all win a pennant and obtain fatter paychecks, Durocher pointed out. Day added that Robinson was "a nice quiet guy that we wouldn't have to associate with off the field."[36] Reese and Higbe agreed to refuse to sign the dump-Robinson petition. Durocher and Rickey then met with the rebellious players and offered to trade them. Bragan and Walker were sent to Pittsburgh, but apparently Walker regretted his decision, returning to the Dodgers and tearing up his letter of resignation. The petition campaign had fizzled out.

Just days later, on April 15, the season opened with the Dodgers playing the Boston Braves at Ebbets Field. There were no incidents until the Dodgers traveled to Philadelphia to play against the Phillies, managed by Alabama-born Ben Chapman. Rickey had advance warning of trouble ahead. The general manager of the Phillies, Herb Pennock, told him, "You just can't bring that nigger here with the rest of your team, Branch. We're just not ready for that sort of thing yet."[37]

Back in the 1930s, when Ben Chapman had played for the New York Yankees, he had razzed Hank Greenberg and other Jewish players with virulently anti-Semitic remarks. Now as Phillies manager, Chapman instructed his players to throw the book of racist epithets at Robinson, "to see if he can take it."[38] The bench jockeying by Chapman's team went far beyond the usual limits. Robinson's teammates were told that they would catch horrible skin diseases if they touched his towels or combs. Under this barrage of insults, Robinson did not play his best, and his future in major-league ball seemed shaky. Fans and journalists inundated Commissioner Chandler with protest let-

*In 1947 Jackie Robinson became the first African American
to play major-league baseball in the twentieth century.*

ters and phone calls. Finally, Chandler warned Chapman to
cease and desist. But the attacks had one substantial side
benefit: some of Robinson's teammates warmed up to him
under the assault. Eddie Stanky publicly labeled Chapman
a coward, and even Dixie Walker protested.

At the time Robinson claimed the insults didn't upset
him, but twenty-five years later he wrote:

This day of all the unpleasant days of my life brought me nearer to cracking up than I have ever been. For one wild and rage-crazed minute I thought "To hell with Mr. Rickey's noble experiment.... [I wanted to] stride over to that Phillies dugout, grab one of those white sons of bitches and smash his teeth with my despised black fist."[39]

Back in New York City, supporters were incensed by the unsportsmanlike behavior of the Phillies. Chapman was pressured to apologize and shake Robinson's hand for the cameras. Robinson was no more eager than Chapman, but he obliged the press.

One more problem Robinson encountered in Philadelphia was his exclusion from the club hotel, the Benjamin Franklin. Robinson was sent off on his own. Sportswriter Jimmy Cannon, covering the event, reported that Robinson was "the loneliest man I have ever seen in sports."[40]

Life on the road was especially difficult. Rickey could have boycotted team hotels that refused to accept Robinson and his wife. Instead, trying not to rock the boat, Rickey accepted the insulting rules of segregation that continued on for more than a decade. Catcher Johnny Roseboro, an African-American player who joined the Dodgers in 1957, criticized the management for acquiescing to the rules of Jim Crow hotels:

At the same time when they signed blacks and Latins, they should have made sure they would be welcome. If the black Dodgers weren't welcome in a motel, hotel, or theater, the white Dodgers should have fought for their rights and walked out. Instead the Dodgers didn't care.[41]

Opposing pitchers seemed hell bent on hitting Robinson—he was hit by pitches seven times by the end of his first season. Robinson's quick reflexes prevented too much damage, and somehow he kept his temper under wraps.

Despite all the pressure, in city after city, Robinson played star-quality baseball. He became a tremendous drawing card, bunting and stealing bases like no other player, to the roars of white and black fans alike. Attendance escalated as African Americans flocked to ballparks. For games in Cincinnati, Ohio, a "Jackie Robinson special train" embarked from faraway Norfolk, Virginia, stopping along the way to pick up black fans. Possibly under advisement from their church leaders, African Americans wore their best Sunday clothing to ball games but they could not stop cheering Robinson every time he came up to bat. If Robinson struck out, low moans washed over the crowd.

Not only in Brooklyn but everywhere, most African Americans and many Latinos became proud Dodger fans. In Brooklyn, Robinson had numerous white fans, people who supported the civil rights alliance. One Jewish New Yorker had fond memories of attending a game at Ebbets Field in 1947:

> During the game Jackie made a good play in the field, at which point everyone was yelling, "Jackie, Jackie, Jackie," and I was yelling with them. And suddenly I realized that behind me someone was yelling, "Yonkel, Yonkel, Yonkel," which is Yiddish for Jackie.... It was a very moving moment. [42]

Despite the increased attendance attributed to Robinson's exciting playing, his salary remained the major-league minimum, $5,000. For months he was not permitted to expand his income by accepting offers from advertisers.

In a *New York Times* interview, Robinson mentioned one opposing player who seemed to go out of his way to support him: Hank Greenberg, then the rival first baseman of the Pittsburgh Pirates. One day, Greenberg approached him at first base after he had been spiked and asked if he was OK. "Stick in there," Robinson quoted Greenberg as saying. "You're doing fine. Keep your chin up."

"Class tells," Robinson told the reporter. "It sticks out

all over Mr. Greenberg." Years later Greenberg recalled the incident in his autobiography and commented:

> *Jackie had it tough, tougher than any ballplayer who ever lived. I happened to be a Jew, one of the few in baseball, but I was white.... I identified with Jackie Robinson, I had feelings for him because they had treated me the same way. Not as bad... I said to Robinson at first base, "Don't pay any attention to these Southern [bench] jockeys. They aren't worth anything as far as you're concerned." He thanked me and I said, "Would you like to go to dinner?" He said, "I'd love to go to dinner, but I shouldn't because it'll put you on the spot."[43]*

To the surprise of no one, the Dodgers won the 1947 pennant, with Robinson hitting .297, leading the league in stolen bases, and being named Rookie of the Year. The New York Yankees beat the Dodgers in the nation's first integrated World Series, 4 games to 3. No one faulted Robinson for the loss. On September 23, a Jackie Robinson Day took place at Ebbets Field. Black celebrities officiated as their hero was showered with gifts.

In 1948, Rickey moved spring training to the Dominican Republic. Dominican fans poured in

> *to see Robinson at bat. Thirteen-year-old Felipe Alou, who someday would play and manage in the major leagues, was in the crowd. Later he said that to see Robinson in the Brooklyn lineup gave us hope ... there was a black man out there with a major league uniform on. He beat us, too. Our Dominican All Stars had the Dodgers beat 2-1 into the ninth when Robinson hit a liner over second with a man on and raced around the bases. How he could fly![44]*

Other Latino and black players hoped that with Robinson's success, the integration of baseball would pick up its pace. In the opinion of black Negro-league veteran and future Hall-of-Famer Monte Irvin, there were "ten, twenty, thirty guys who could just step right in." Although Irvin was hired by the New York Giants in 1949, it took until 1959 before the color line was finally dropped by all the major-league teams. More often than not, Latino players became the owners' preferred choice over equally qualified African-American ones.

In mid-1947 Bill Veeck's Cleveland Indians signed up twenty-two-year-old African-American outfielder Larry Doby of the Newark Eagles. Veeck paid Effa Manley $10,000 for Doby and brought him straight to Cleveland, bypassing the farm-team route. No other team moved to integrate.

In 1948 a few teams signed on black players, most of them going off to farm teams. Yankee general manager Larry MacPhail would not budge even in the direction of integrating minor-league baseball. He still insisted he could not find talented prospects. Negro-league players watched, waited, and grew more and more discouraged, especially older players like Satchel Paige. When Veeck signed Doby, he received a telegram from Paige. "Is it time for me to come?"

At first Veeck was concerned that if he brought Paige to Cleveland, it would be called a publicity gimmick. But by July the Indians were in a three-way tie for second place and needed a pitcher badly. Veeck paid a full-year's salary to acquire Paige for the remaining three months of the season. Seventy-two thousand fans came to watch Paige win the game, putting the Indians into a four-way tie for first place. Whites and blacks enthusiastically cheered Paige on. Later Veeck was forced to drop Paige for his constant habit of violating curfews, absenteeism, and lateness. But no one ever forgot the legendary old-timer's shining moment with the major leagues.

Four other black players were added to the Dodgers. As expected they were Newcombe, Campanella, Partlow, and Wright. The Negro leagues lost money after 1947. Only the

East-West game drew decent audiences for a few years. Unwelcome in the majors, nonwhite players headed for the Mexican League, which was then paying good salaries (see chapter 5).

In 1949 the Dodgers announced that spring training would take place in Atlanta, Georgia. Jackie Robinson hated the South. In Macon, Georgia, he and Campanella stayed with a black family in a private home as a Ku Klux Klan cross burned across the street. Robinson, the symbol of baseball's integration, had obeyed Branch Rickey's rules for two seasons. Now, for the 1949 season, he took off the wraps and warned racists like Phillies manager Ben Chapman "If you open your mouth one more time...." The press viewed the new Robinson as "a swelled head wise guy, an uppity nigger."[45]

It was Robinson's best season, perhaps because he no longer held in his feelings. He scored 122 runs, drove in 124, and led the league in stolen bases with 37 and in batting at .342. Named Most Valuable Player, Robinson and Rookie of the Year Don Newcombe led the '49 Dodgers to the pennant. Improved because they were judging players on performance instead of skin color, the Dodgers captured seven pennants and one World Series between 1947 and 1956. In 1952 they hired Cuban outfielder Sandy Amoros. Willie Mays had joined the rival New York Giants a year earlier.

Despite the publicity and added gate receipts whenever a dark-skinned Latino or African American joined a major-league team, after 1951 ten out of sixteen teams remained segregated. To some it seemed that hiring standards remained cemented in skin pigmentation. Character, personality, and lifestyle of nonwhite baseball players were investigated with far greater care than ever was accorded white players.

One Mexican player, Roberto Avila, a second baseman for the Cuban League, described by sportswriters as "one of the swarthier Mexicans,"[46] became the first dark-

Cleveland's Roberto Avila turns a double play. The Mexican second baseman was the first dark-skinned Latino to play in the newly integrated major leagues and the first Latino to win a batting title, with a .341 average in 1954.

skinned Latino to play in the newly integrated major leagues. He was signed by Bill Veeck, Jr., to play second base on the Cleveland Indians in 1949. The press renamed him "Bobby" Avila, a pattern of Anglicizing Latino names that persists today. Avila led the American League in batting in 1954 with an average of .341. Cleveland traded Avila away in 1958 when he was thirty-four years old, and he retired a year later. Later, Cleveland brought him back as a scout, and he discovered such talents at Luis Tiant, Jr. (see chapter 7).

The 1954 pennant-winning Cleveland Indians were a team that featured multicultural cooperation. It was managed by Al López, who had been hired by general manager Hank Greenberg. It starred Avila, Doby, and African-American Luke Easter and Jewish-American Al Rosen. A California-born Latino named Edward Miguel "Mike" García (19–7, with a league-leading 2.64 ERA) anchored a pitching staff that included 23-game winners Bob Lemon and Early Wynn. Cleveland won an all-time major-league record 111 games that year.

When Cleveland failed to win another pennant, however, the owners let go of Avila, Rosen, Doby, and García. They fired Hall-of-Famer Greenberg and future Hall-of-Famer López. Greenberg's hiring of black and Latino players, as well as Jewish ones like Rosen and catcher Myron Ginsberg, did not sit well with other baseball executives. Greenberg never was hired by another club. The Cleveland team did not return to its glory days until 1994–95, when once again it became a multicultural giant, sparked by a lineup that was half Latino (see chapter 9).

Havana-born Saturnino Orestes Arrieta Armas became the blackest Latino yet to integrate baseball. He used his stepfather's name, Miñoso, and became known as Minnie Miñoso. An ardent baseball fan, he grew up in Cuba organizing games at every sugar plantation where he and the rest of his family went to cut cane. By 1944 he was playing professional baseball for the Club Marianao of the Cuban

Winter League and was named Rookie of the Year. In 1945 he joined the New York Cubans of the Negro league and played on the All-Star team. His roommate was Silvio García, the man Rickey had rejected earlier.

Already in his late twenties when Robinson joined the Dodgers, Miñoso spent two seasons with a Cleveland Indians farm team in the heavily Latino city of San Diego and then was traded to the Chicago White Sox in 1951. There, he was joined by Venezuelan shortstop "Chico" Carrasquel. The colorful Cuban took the Windy City by storm, hitting .326 and leading the league in stolen bases and triples. He finished second in the league in batting and third in slugging average. Chicago's attendance skyrocketed by half a million that year, as fans chanted "Go, Go!" every time Miñoso got on base. Overnight, the White Sox became known as the "Go-Go Sox."

Minnie Miñoso also won a less sought-after record during his rookie year—topping the charts of those struck with beanballs. The previous year, Easter and Rosen set the record when each was hit ten times. By the end of the season, Miñoso had been hit a whopping 16 times and at the end of four seasons, 65 times, 8 times in his head! In 1956, Frank Robinson, later to become baseball's first African-American manager, was hit 20 times. (Before managing in the majors, Frank Robinson spent five years managing a team in the Puerto Rican Winter League.)

Miñoso, who spoke English with a heavy accent, was always quoted in news reports with a phonetic transcription of his accent, something not done for Southerners and others who had their own speech patterns. Miñoso discussed his record as a beanball target with a *Sporting News* writer, and his interview was written up in a mocking dialect reserved for Latinos: "I theenk I wear a headguard even in bed. Maybe somebody throw at me when I sleep too. I don't know whatta kind of baseball this is. Yes, you try to get a man out. You brushback. But you do not try to keel him."[47]

Miñoso compiled a lifetime major-league average of

Cuban-born Minnie Moñoso rounds third for the Chicago White Sox. He later became baseball's only five-decade player and the oldest player to hit safely in a major-league game.

.298. He later served as a White Sox coach. Occasionally picking up the bat to play in a game, he became baseball's only five-decade player, as well as the oldest player to hit safely.

Miñoso blazed the trail for dozens of other Cuban major leaguers, including shortstop Leo "Chico" Cardenas, outfielder Sandy Amoros, and pitching aces Pedro "Preston" Gómez, Camilo Pascual, and Sandy Consuegra. They were soon followed by such Cuban stars as Bert Campaneris, Mike Cuellar, Tony Oliva, Tony Pérez, José Tartabull (father of slugger Danny Tartabull), and Luis Tiant, Jr. (see chapter 7).

In the late 1940s and early 1950s, unemployed Negro leaguers, many of whom had never earned a living at anything but baseball, went job hunting, finding work in assembly plants, the post office, and as security guards. A few lucky ones stayed close to baseball, working as scouts and trainers. They were proud of the few who had made it to the majors: Jackie Robinson, Frank Robinson, Hank Aaron, Roy Campanella, Willie Mays, Elston Howard, Monte Irvin, Joe Black, Don Newcombe, Larry Doby, and Minnie Miñoso.

It would be several years more before a massive civil rights movement would begin to reverse Jim Crow and due credit would begin to be awarded some of the African American and Latino Negro-league old-timers for their outstanding playing of America's national pastime. But by the early 1950s it appeared to many that the few lucky blacks and Latinos who were making it into major-league baseball might be the last to do so.

5
cinco

MEXICAN LEAGUE AND FIRST HALL-OF-FAMER

It is harder for a Puerto Rican or Latin ballplayer. People do not want to give them any work off the field [making advertising commercials]. So no one knows them. I would make a lot more money in baseball if I were a white American.
— Roberto Clemente[1]

After 1950 the uproar over the integration of baseball quieted down to a whisper and then disappeared, despite the fact that so many teams remained lily white. A sharp escalation of the Cold War silenced most people who would have continued to fight back. Persons discussing the issue of civil rights were labeled "Communists" and found themselves hounded and even fired from their jobs. The U.S. attorney general issued a list of "subversive" organizations threatening American democracy. High on the list was the Committee to End Jim Crow in Baseball!

Because of Harry Truman's civil rights statements, African Americans had helped elect him president in 1948. But after he issued an executive order for military integration, he quickly dropped the issue of racial equality, and the Army brass defied the order. A handful of African Americans received appointments to federal posts, but the lynchings and racial segregation did not end.

The economy went into a tailspin in the late 1940s. Then the Korean War (1950–53) sent it soaring again, as defense industries boomed. Korea had divided into two countries after World War II: North Korea under Soviet and Chinese influence, South Korea dominated by the United States. U.S. troops were sent off to fight alongside the South Koreans against North Korean and, eventually, Chinese troops. Few dared to protest. The war ended in a stalemate, with the old boundary between North and South Korea still in place. But 2 million Koreans and 34,000 Americans lay dead in their graves.[2]

The only good news that came out of the Korean conflict was the racial integration of American troops fighting the war, brought about when the Chinese almost drove U.S. white battalions into the sea and black reinforcements had to be thrown into combat. Also, the economy recovered during the war, but not to the benefit of the majority of Latinos and African Americans. They continued to suffer from severe housing and job discrimination.

When the recession returned at war's end, a scapegoat

Illegal Mexican immigrants are captured by immigration officials in Los Angeles. During the 1953 Operation Wetback, the U.S. government returned more than a million Mexican immigrants—approximately a third of whom were American citizens—to Mexico.

was needed for the lack of jobs for returning war veterans. The targets this time were Mexican immigrant workers. Agents of the Immigration and Naturalization Service and other law officers invaded their neighborhoods and workplaces in a scandalous federally sponsored roundup known as "Operation Wetback." More than a million men, women, and children were herded into rail cars and shipped off to Mexico, without even a hearing. As many as a third of them were U.S. citizens.

All this was happening at a time when major-league owners were trying to bring Mexican baseball owners to heel before their dictates. They had been stung by the Mexicans in the 1940s when several of their players had jumped to the Mexican Baseball League for higher pay. The owners had since signed restrictive agreements with all the other Latin American baseball nations except Mexico.

The ill will had deep historical roots in the history of the two countries' relations, dating as far back as the creation of Texas in the 1830s and the U.S.-Mexico War of 1846–48. Overnight, the treaty ending that war converted some 100,000 Mexicans residing in the Southwest into U.S. citizens. They had little time for baseball: they were too busy dealing with the white "Anglo" settlers who took their farms and mines through legal trickery and armed violence.

By the 1870s Mexican Americans were joining thousands of imported Mexican workers to build the nation's railroads, dig out the copper from the mines, and harvest crops in lands that had once been their own. In the mining camps they were segregated into areas called "Jim towns." They worked at what was called "the Mexican wage," or half of what whites were paid, and for longer hours.

Modern-style baseball had been popular in Mexico ever since it was introduced by Cubans and Americans in the late nineteenth century. During the thirty-five-year dictatorship (1876–1911) in Mexico of Porfirio Díaz, U.S. rail, mining, and oil tycoons brought in American workers to supervise low-paid Mexican workers. Sometimes the Americans played baseball with "the locals." Racism was a constant hassle, though. As the wealthy oil mogul Edward L. Doheny pointed out, the Americans "carried arms" and treated Mexicans with "a domineering spirit."[3]

The Mexican Revolution of 1910–20 replaced baseballs with bullets. At some of the mines, former worker-players attacked their American supervisors. Before it was all over, some two million Mexicans had lost their lives in a raging civil war, and the United States had invaded Mexico twice.

The Mexican Baseball League did not stabilize until the early 1920s. Its teams played exhibition games against Negro-league teams and occasional major-league teams. Mexican teams also barnstormed in Texas and the Southwest. A few Mexican stars played U.S. major-league ball. One was Baldomero Melo "Mel" Almada. In a seven-year major-league career that started in 1933, Almada batted .284.

During the 1930s and 1940s, Mexican, Venezuelan, and Caribbean Basin summer leagues, in general, attracted not only black players but white ones as well. This was usually because they paid better salaries and offered a less racist atmosphere. By the early 1940s, Veracruz millionaire Jorge Pasquel and his four brothers were hiring Negro-league stars like Josh Gibson, Willie Wells, Roy Campanella, Monte Irvin, and Buck Leonard to play in the six-team Mexican Baseball League. They treated the men well, even hiring tutors for their children.

When two African-American players in Mexico were drafted by the United States to help fight the Nazis in World War II, Jorge Pasquel got them back by arranging a "trade." He used his government contacts to arrange a loan of 80,000 Mexican workers to the United states in exchange for the two players. This deal was a little-known part of the rapidly growing "Bracero Program" created in 1942 in a bilateral treaty that was interrupted by 1954's "Operation Wetback" and did not officially end until 1964. The bracero treaty provided Mexican workers to help keep the United States' railroads, mines, and farms running at full capacity. Its chief U.S. administrator later called the Bracero Program "legalized slavery."[4]

After World War II ended, Pasquel feasted his eyes on

Mexican League president Jorge Pasquel (right) watches a league game in 1946. Pasquel caused a stir by luring leading Latino and several white players from the U.S. major leagues.

all the Latino players in the United States who would lose their jobs to the white players returning from the war. He became Mexican League president and expanded the league to eight teams. To fill the new rosters, he recruited leading Latino major leaguers who faced likely demotion to the minors, including Puerto Rican outfielder Luis Olmo of the Brooklyn Dodgers. He brought fifty-six-year-old Dolf Luque from Cuba to manage the Puebla team.

Some thirteen white players grabbed the lucrative salaries offered by Pasquel, jumping to the Mexican Baseball League. They included stars like catcher Mickey Owen, shortstop Vern Stephens, and pitcher Sal "the Barber" Maglie. Pasquel boasted he would soon be inviting super-stars Ted Williams, Joe DiMaggio, Stan Musial, and Hank Greenberg. Williams's mother was part Mexican American and part French American, making him one-fourth Mexican. He had batted .406 in 1941 and was burning up baseball as its top hitter of the 1940s and 1950s.[5]

Baseball commissioner Chandler ruled that players who jumped to Mexico would be banned from U.S. baseball if they did not return by the start of the 1946 season. U.S. players benefited from the Mexican League's "raids." They began organizing to demand better pay, forming the American Baseball Guild, forerunner of the players' union of today. The Guild won a $5,000 minimum salary and a pension plan. The players then threatened antitrust suits unless their banished teammates in Mexico were allowed back into organized baseball. Chandler backed down in 1949 and permitted the jumpers to return. Maglie, his pitching polished by Luque's tips, came home to win 59 games for the New York Giants from 1950 to 1953.

U.S. baseball made sure there would be no repeat effort. As early as 1948, the major leagues began signing deals with the Caribbean leagues to regulate the movement of players and to institutionalize winter baseball. The Caribbean leagues became today's "free testing ground" for major-league teams' prospective players, a relationship subsequently "formalized with a ban against hiring players with more than a hundred days' experience in the majors."[6]

In 1948 the first Latin American championship series was organized. Participating teams came from Cuba, Panama, Venezuela, and Puerto Rico. Given the name Caribbean World Series a year later, it provided U.S. baseball scouts an opportunity for a closer look at leading Latin American players. U.S. minor leagues president George

Trautman threw out the first pitch for the first year's Series in Havana, won by Cuba's Almendares team, managed by Fermín "Mike" Guerra, the Havana-born catcher of the Philadelphia A's. The Almendares team included major leaguers Al Gionfriddo, Monte Irvin, and Sam Jethroe in the outfield. Not infrequently, other U.S. stars, including Willie Mays, played in the Caribbean World Series. The Series momentarily ended in 1960 when the United States broke relations with Cuba because of the revolution there (see chapter 7).

The Mexican League, despite its attractions, did not do well financially. During the Mexican "raiding party" of the 1940s, the Pasquels had overplayed their hand. They did not have large enough stadiums to meet the demand for tickets, and they lost out on some of their other financial investments.

Still it was not so easy for the owners of U.S. clubs to impose the Caribbean-type arrangements on a big country like Mexico. In 1955, Jorge Pasquel died in a plane crash. As Operation Wetback wound down, a U.S.-Mexico baseball agreement was reached. The Mexican summer league became part of the U.S. minor-league system, but its teams were not bound to any major-league organization. A major-league team had to purchase the contract of a Mexican player, a practice that continues today. To discourage any more potential Sal Maglies, Mexican clubs were limited to no more than two U.S. players per team.

Most of the time, Mexican owners kept the prices of their players high, discouraging U.S. buyers. Even so, some forty Mexican players entered the majors after 1955. But, in

*Dr. Arturo Benogochea, president of the
Cuban delegation, holds the 1958 Carribean
World Series trophy after the Cuban team
won the series for the third straight year.*

light of widespread racism and anti-Mexican prejudices in the United States, many players, like home-run king Héctor Espino, chose to stay home.

Espino briefly played for a Los Angeles Dodgers farm team in 1964 in Jacksonville, Florida, and reportedly was miserable. The man who scouted him, former Havana Sugar Kings owner and famed baseball promoter Bobby Maduro (see chapter 6), noted that the Mexican long-ball hitter "couldn't adjust to things here, the food, the manner of living, anything."[7] Espino became a national hero in Mexico in 1965 when he refused to join the St. Louis Cardinals after they bought his contract from the Monterrey Sultans. Instead, he played twenty-four years in Mexico, where he hit 760 home runs, twice batted over .400, and ended his career with a .330 average and 18 batting titles. Loved by Mexicans, he lived a happy and comfortable life, never having to worry about becoming a migrant worker in a foreign land.

Meanwhile, ten out of sixteen baseball clubs still maintained segregation in 1953. At the end of the 1953 season, the New York Yankees finally broke their color barrier and placed African-American Elston Howard and Puerto Rican Vic Power on their team roster. Like Minnie Miñoso, Power came from a very poor family. His father died when he was only thirteen years old. At age sixteen Power went to work in a sugarcane factory to help his seamstress mother. Like Miñoso too, Power played ball whenever he found a few others willing to pitch or hit. By 1947 he was playing professional baseball in the Puerto Rican League for a salary of $250 a month. Spotted by a Yankee scout, he was sent to play on a farm team in Canada and was never actually allowed to play for the Yankees.

The Yankees chose the mild-mannered Howard as their token black man instead, even though Power had the better batting average. Some said it was because Power brooked no insults, fought back, reportedly dated white women, and was, as he himself acknowledged later, "the original showboat hot dog."[8] In December 1953 the Yankees traded Power to the Philadelphia A's. In twelve seasons with six major-league teams, Power batted .284.

Power was shocked by segregation in the United States. In Puerto Rico, restaurants would serve a meal to anyone with the money to pay for it. Power asked teammate Gary Bird for an explanation of the situation in the South, and Bird answered, "Vic, it's been like that for a hundred years an' we gonna keep it like that." Power told one writer:

> *I have to travel in the same bus with the guys, an' they stop on the road so they can go eating. An' I can't go in. But they never brought me a sandwich or a hamburger! I just stayed in the bus waiting and after they ate, they came in, nobody brought me nothing. An' they were my friends. An' we played together. But they were very cold.*

To water down the hurt, Power sometimes told jokes about his experiences, the most famous being, "I tried to eat in the restaurant an' the lady told me, 'Sorry, we don't serve Negroes.' I tol' her, "I don't wanna eat Negro, I want some rice and beans.'"[9]

Jokes aside, Vic Power never got over his experience with U.S. baseball. "When I first went to the major leagues, they were throwing beanballs. An' we don't use no helmets or nothin'!" he said. "In baseball, you have to fight back.... You have to let them respect you."[10]

Civil rights cases had been laboriously proceeding through the court system for decades. The best Latinos or African Americans could do was an occasional local court victory. Finally, on May 17, 1954, the Supreme Court ruled in *Brown v. the Board of Education*, that segregation in public schools was unconstitutional. Because the case was specifically directed at African Americans, Latinos were not officially covered by *Brown* until 1973![11]

Few could have predicted the storm of hatred and violence that spread across the South for the next decade.

There broke out a rash of beatings, shootings, and even murders of black people attempting to register their children in all-white schools. Latino and black baseball players saw travel conditions rapidly worsen. Death threats against dark-skinned players were also not unusual. Hank Aaron and Puerto Rican Félix Mantilla, hired by Milwaukee in 1954 and 1956, respectively, to bring the Braves a pennant and the World Series championship in 1957, received death threats in Montgomery, Alabama. Years later, in 1974, when he broke Babe Ruth's record for career home runs, Aaron had to hire a bodyguard because of all the death threats.

Logically, the Supreme Court decision should have convinced all baseball owners to open their doors wide for black and Latino players, but no such thing occurred. Not a word was heard from the Philadelphia Phillies, the Detroit Tigers, or the Boston Red Sox. For all of the 1950s only 8 percent of major-league players were African Americans or dark-skinned Latinos, most of them hired at the end of the decade when the Civil Rights Movement was moving into high gear.

As Vic Power had noticed, few white players were conscious of the humiliation faced by their darker-skinned teammates. Even Hank Greenberg did not realize the gravity of the situation. One day in 1955, when his team got off the bus after a long ride, Greenberg noticed five black players standing around instead of jumping into taxis to head for the team's hotel. When he asked them what was going on, for the first time he realized that his dark-skinned players stayed in private homes because they were not welcome at the team's downtown hotel. When Greenberg wrote to the hotels and threatened to boycott them, they changed their policies.

In 1957, the Philadelphia Phillies finally hired shortstop John Kennedy from the dying Kansas City Monarchs and Humberto "Chico" Fernández, a Cuban-born twenty-five-year-old shortstop, who had been hired by the Dodgers the previous year. Kennedy was quickly dumped back into the minors after a shoulder injury, and Fernández took over the starting shortstop position.

The Detroit Tigers refused to budge, although there were plenty of candidates in their farm system. Finally, a civil rights group, the Briggs Stadium Boycott Committee, declared that they would organize a boycott of Tiger games if the situation were not rectified. In 1958 the Tigers added Puerto Rican third baseman Ozzie Virgil to their roster, acquired during a trade with the Giants. Virgil's son grew up to be a catcher for the Phillies and Braves in the 1980s.

By 1959 fifteen teams had integrated, most in a tokenistic way. Only the Boston Red Sox refused to move. Starting with one picket at Fenway Park daring to carry a sign reading "Race Hate is Killing Baseball in Boston," the effort to complete integration moved forward. Jackie Robinson condemned the Red Sox during a speech in Boston. The NAACP and Ministerial Alliance of Greater Boston urged the Massachusetts Commission against Discrimination to investigate the baseball club, pointing out that there were also no blacks or Latinos employed at Fenway Park in other capacities. The commission held a hearing but cleared the team of bias charges when promises to correct the situation were made. One player, infielder Elijah "Pumpsie" Green, was brought up from the minors to fulfill the promise.

By the late 1950s, as the growing Civil Rights Movement in the South attracted national attention, black and Latino players began pushing harder for changed conditions during spring training in Florida. St. Petersburg was the training ground for both the St. Louis Cardinals and the Yankees, and the city benefited greatly from the tourist business the teams attracted. The players' union, rebaptized in 1953 as the Major League Baseball Players Association, formally protested hotel segregation and demanded that club owners pressure team hotels. The Yankees moved to Fort Lauderdale where hotels promised to provide housing for the entire team. Not wanting to lose baseball business completely, St. Petersburg removed its hotel segregation codes, at least for the Cardinals and newly formed New York Mets. Latinos and blacks who lived in the city year-round, of course, were not so lucky.

As late as 1963, Jackie Robinson, who had retired in 1957, was calling on baseball owners to "enact a rule demanding equal accommodations and services to all players at all times."[12] And still organized baseball dragged its feet. But as the Civil Rights Movement spread from the South to the rest of the country, the experiment that began with Jackie Robinson began picking up steam. The 1960s would witness an entirely new ball game. By then, one Latino-black outfielder would stand out above all other major-league players, white or nonwhite: Roberto Clemente.

Hired by Pittsburgh in 1955, Clemente became the first Latino ever voted into the Hall of Fame. For most baseball writers and fans he remains to this day in a class all his own. His African-American Pirates teammate and fellow Hall-of-Famer, Willie Stargell, later recalled him as "the finest all-around player in the major leagues."[13]

In 18 seasons, during which he frequently played with injuries to his back, shoulders, or legs, Clemente compiled a lifetime batting average of .317 and a slugging average of .475. Yet those were the years when fastball and "control" pitching became the name of the game, and baseball batting averages wilted. Clemente was one of the few players in baseball history ever to win four batting titles. He was the only player in history to hit safely in every World Series game in which he played. He also was the first player in the twentieth century to whack ten hits in two consecutive games, against the Dodgers at the height of the sizzling 1970 pennant race. Like so many Latino stars, Clemente could do it all. Known for his cannonball throws from the outfield, he won a dozen Gold Glove awards, including six consecutive ones (1961–66).

Still going strong at age thirty-eight, Clemente batted .312 in 1972, his eighteenth big-league season. He entered that summer's next-to-last game looking for his 3,000th base hit. It would place him in the company of ten other baseball immortals, including his African-American contemporaries Willie Mays (third in lifetime home runs) and Hank Aaron (who broke Ruth's home-run record three years later).

A hush fell over the expectant crowd that day when Clemente stepped to the plate. Then Clemente leaned into a curveball from New York Met southpaw Jon Matlack and lined it off the left center-field wall for a stand-up double—his 3,000th career base hit. Fans rose to their feet and kept up their wild cheering until Clemente doffed his batting helmet to them.

Roberto's father, Melchor Clemente, was a sugarcane mill worker. Roberto's mother, Luisa Walker Clemente, worked as a cleaning lady. Clemente never forgot his father's pointing to the boss driving a fancy car and saying, "He is no better than you."[14] Like so many Puerto Ricans, young Roberto loved baseball. By age fourteen he was playing sandlot games using a stick for a bat and a tin can for a ball. His talent was obvious to rice salesman Roberto Marín, scouting for his employer's softball team. "He never struck out. Bam! Bam! Bam! Tin cans all over the field."[15] Marín gave Roberto a Sello Rojo rice company uniform.

By the time he was seventeen, Roberto's talents had attracted the eye of a part-time scout for the Brooklyn Dodgers, Pedrín Zorilla, owner of the Santurce Cangrejeros (Crabbers). Zorilla invited the Dodgers' chief Latin American scout, Al Campanis, to have a look at Clemente in open tryouts. Campanis was enormously impressed, but the majors could not legally hire a high school player without his parents' consent. Roberto's father signed a Dodgers contract with an X. Later, the Milwaukee Braves tripled the Dodgers' offer of a $5,000 annual salary and $10,000 bonus, and Roberto asked his mother for advice. "You must keep your word," she said.

The Dodgers shipped Roberto to Montreal. They tried to prevent scouts from noticing him by keeping him on the Montreal bench as much as possible. During the winter of 1954–55, he led Santurce, a team that included Willie Mays and other big-league stars, to its third consecutive Caribbean World Series championship.

But the Dodgers couldn't hide such a great talent as Clemente's from a man like wily Branch Rickey, then Pittsburgh Pirates president. At a time when white ballplayers were demanding handsome bonuses to sign, Rickey sent his chief scout, Howie Haak, to look for less expensive Latino players. Haak was glad he no longer had to have Cubans sign "this phony form sayin' they were of white ancestry."[16] Haak spotted Clemente right away. Draft rules gave the lowest finishing teams first choice, and so the Pirates, perennial last-place finishers, drafted Clemente, who recalled "I didn't even know where Pittsburgh was."[17]

At least it was not in the racially segregated South. Even so, Roberto quickly discovered racism thrived in the North too. As he later told 44,000 fans, mostly Puerto Ricans, at the Mets' Shea Stadium for a Roberto Clemente Night: "In the early days, segregation baffled us.... The people who never run into these problems don't have any idea at all what kind of an ordeal this can be."[18]

Clemente's .311 average and other impressive stats in 1956 caused Rickey again to send Haak to several Latin American countries. Over the next few decades, Haak signed dozens of Latino stars, including Panamanian second baseman Rennie Stennett (lifetime batting average .274), Venezuelan outfielder Tony Armas (.252), and Dominican catcher Tony Peña (.273).

Clemente's spectacular play year after year helped lead the Pirates out of the cellar and all the way to a World Series championship in 1960. Yet baseball writers, many of them disturbed by the rising number of Latinos and blacks in the majors, refused to vote Clemente the Most Valuable Player (MVP) award. In protest, Roberto refused to wear his World Series ring.

For most of his career, Clemente was much appreciated by discerning fans but was not treated with much respect by baseball officialdom or the press. Sportswriters refused to use his real first name in their stories, calling him "Bob" or "Bobby" instead. Clemente suffered the double racial prejudice traditionally dished out to blacks and Latinos. One writer infuriated him by calling him in print a "Puerto Rican hot dog." Another said he was not a "team player." Still others applied the standard Latino stereotype to him, calling him "hot-tempered" and "emotional." Many ridiculed him as a "hypochondriac," a charge often leveled at him by his manager, Danny Murtaugh.

From the beginning Clemente fought back. He regularly denounced sportswriters, opponents, and even teammates for their acts of racism. When white teammates shouted racial slurs at black opponents, he and Cuban teammate Román Mejías "challenged the rest of the team right in the dugout—a lot of the players didn't like us because we were not white."[19] When his accent was ridiculed in the press, Clemente told reporters to start learning some Spanish.

In 1964, ten years after entering U.S. baseball, Roberto Clemente married Vera Cristina Zabala, a bank employee back in Puerto Rico. He moved with Vera to a spacious new house in Rio Piedras, a middle-class suburb outside San Juan. The Clementes' three sons were all born on the island at Roberto's insistence. He bought a home nearby for his parents. Clemente never lost sight of his roots in the barrio. He often passed his off-season time making ceramics, envisioning a national ceramics cottage industry as a possible help in overcoming Puerto Rico's unemployment problems. He also began planning a huge sports complex for the capital city of San Juan. It would be called Ciudad Deportiva, or Sports City, and would be free to all people, with an emphasis on recreation for poor children.

Clemente often complained to his wife, Vera, about the bad press given Latinos: "They make a good play, the press don't mention them. They do something bad, they put it on the first page!"[20] During the feverish 1966 pennant race, Roberto patiently explained to the very reporters who so abused him:

> *The Latin American player doesn't get the recognition he deserves. Neither does the Negro player, unless he does something really spectacular, like Willie Mays. We have self-satisfaction, yes. But after the season is over, nobody cares about us.... Juan Marichal [of the Dominican Republic] is one of the greatest pitchers in the game, but does he get invited to banquets? Somebody says we live too far away. That's a lousy excuse. I am an American citizen. But some people act like they think I live in the jungle someplace. To those people, we are outsiders, foreigners.* [21]

Not until the year 1966, when he passed the 2,000-hit mark and drove in 119 runs, did Roberto Clemente finally win the National League's MVP honor. By then his spectacular hitting, 360-degree spins in the outfield, and bullet throws to home plate were legend.

Clemente was also given the Most Valuable Player Award for his one-of-a-kind performance in the 1971 World Series: .414 batting average; .759 slugging average; 12 hits, including 2 homers and a triple; and 2 miracle catches in the outfield. Afterwards, he faced the TV cameras and became the first Latino player ever to speak Spanish before a mass TV audience in the United States:

> *Before I say anything, I want to say something in Spanish to my mother and father. En este, el momento*

The great Clemente awaits his turn at bat. Roberto Clemente, the pride of Puerto Rico, was the first Latino to reach the 3,000-hit plateau, and he became the first Latino voted into the Hall of Fame— three months after his death in December 1972.

más grande de mi vida, les pido la benedición. [At this, the greatest moment of my life, I ask your blessing.][22]

Baseball fans felt Clemente was unique in his appreciation of the people without whom baseball as a business would collapse: the fans themselves. He once said: "I believe we owe something to the people who watch us. They work hard for their money."[23] And he liked to interrupt a dull interview by saying: "I love the poor people, the workers, the minority people, the ones who suffer. They have a different outlook on life."[24]

When Pittsburgh fans organized a Roberto Clemente Night in 1970, they introduced a delegation from Puerto Rico carrying a scroll with 300,000 signatures of island residents. After the game, Clemente shed tears, explaining that "If it wasn't for these fans, I don't know what would have happened to me."[25]

How Roberto Clemente was viewed by the rest of the world changed dramatically in December 1972. Two days before Christmas a devastating earthquake rocked Nicaragua, destroying downtown Managua and taking thousands of lives. Clemente, who had been in Nicaragua the previous month, managing the Puerto Rican team in the Mundiales, instantly started relief efforts in Puerto Rico for the earthquake victims, personally going door to door in Río Piedras asking for donations. By the end of the week he had enough supplies to fill an old DC-7 cargo plane donated by a San Juan company.

Roberto wanted to go to Nicaragua with the supplies himself, because he knew the dictator of that country, General Anastasio Somoza, was funneling off earthquake relief aid for himself and his corrupt cronies. He had already received a telephone call from Somoza informing him that only "money and food" would be accepted. When the DC-7's departure on New Year's Eve was delayed because of mechanical problems, Roberto's friends and his wife Vera begged him not to go. "Babies are dying there," he said. "They need these supplies. I'll go down and distribute the supplies myself."[26]

Finally, after 9 P.M., the plane managed to take off, with Roberto and four others aboard. Suddenly, one engine sputtered and the pilot radioed that he was turning back to San Juan. Witnesses saw the plane bank to the left and plummet into the ocean. Divers later found the remains of the pilot but no trace of Clemente. After five days of diving, Clemente's friend and teammate Manny Sanguillén, the free-swinging Panamanian catcher who made an art of hitting bad pitches (lifetime batting average .296), gave up the search, having seen too many large sharks to believe there was any hope.

A nation mourned and the inauguration day for a newly elected governor was postponed. Puerto Rico's governor-elect said: "Our people have lost one of their great glories."[27] Donations poured in for Clemente's pet project, Ciudad Deportiva, a reality today.

Ironically, Nicaragua's dictator used some of the funds from the earthquake aid to rebuild Somoza Stadium, a 30,000-seat baseball facility destroyed by the earthquake. After the Nicaraguan Revolution of 1979 toppled the Somoza dynasty, Nicaraguans honored Clemente by naming a baseball stadium in Masaya after him.

Clemente's tragic death stunned baseball enthusiasts around the world. Baseball officials waived the normal waiting period of five years after a player's last game to allow baseball writers to vote Roberto Clemente into the Hall of Fame on March 20, 1973. It was almost a symbolic act of contrition by U.S. baseball and the press. Honoring Clemente partially made up for the shabby treatment given not only to him but to scores of other dark-skinned Latinos.

The Commissioner's Award, traditionally given to exemplary players, was given a new name: the Roberto Clemente Award, in recognition of the late hero's humanitarian work. Those who knew Clemente best say it was what

Roberto most would have wanted. It was as if something special went out of baseball with Roberto's passing. Many Latino friends and fans still say, *"Me hace falta Roberto Clemente."* And a huge number of non–Spanish-speaking fans still think the same thing in English: "I miss Roberto Clemente."

6

REVOLUTIONIZING

BASEBALL

I can't remember ever being called a racial name in Panama.
— Batting champion Rod Carew[1]

If you are Latin and black and want to be a coach, you also have to be an Uncle Tom; you have to say yes to everything.
— Orlando Cepeda[2]

After the early sensational play of Miñoso and Clemente, major-league team owners began to compete for Latin American talents. Then recruitment of Latino players moved into high gear in the late 1950s and early 1960s, when a powerful Civil Rights Movement challenged Jim Crow.

Americans reacted strongly when they saw on their television screens southern governors blocking school entrances to black children and police unleashing snarling dogs and poking electric cattle prods at peaceful protestors. Facing a nationwide outcry and millions of demonstrators marching in the streets, Congress finally passed strong Civil Rights Acts in 1964 and 1965, barring discrimination in housing and hiring. Presidential orders and court decrees further called for "affirmative action" in implementing the Civil Rights Acts. To make up for centuries of unfairness, "minorities," including women, would sometimes have to be given preferential treatment.

Baseball scouts fanned out across the Caribbean Basin. In the Dominican Republic they became known as "black-catchers." They routinely lied to prospective stars and their parents, "cheating them, or worse, even sequestering them."[3] Some scouts became managers of Latin American teams in order to keep an eye out for emerging talents. A Cincinnati scout was managing the Aragua team in Venezuela when he spotted a teenaged shortstop, David Ismael Concepción. He signed him on the spot, telling him "no club gives bonuses to Latin players."[4] In fact, Concepción had to shell out $44 for a glove and some shoes before he left for the United States.

Nicknamed *"Flaco"* ("Skinny") by teammate Tony Pérez, Dave Concepción played nineteen seasons and helped lead the Reds to four World Series and two World Championships between 1970 and 1976. Sportswriters called him the third great Latino shortstop, following in the footsteps of fellow Venezuelans "Chico" Carrasquel and Luis Aparicio, Jr. (see below).

In the 1980s and 1990s Latino baseball players who

had become scouts or managers tried to put an end to the abuse of young Latino players. Future Manager of the Year Felipe Alou *told Sports Illustrated* in 1981:

> *They sign 25 guys and maybe only one is a good player. It's like they throw a net in the ocean, hoping that maybe they'll get a big fish. The problem is, if they don't get a big fish, they'll throw all the smaller ones back.* [5]

In 1984 a seventeen-year-old minimum age limit was established for Latino players signing with a major-league club.

In an effort to attract the attention of all the scouts "south of the border," future U.S. stars have often lined up to play Caribbean winter ball. Fans in the Dominican Republic, for example, were among the first to cheer the exploits of such future greats as Willie Stargell, Frank Howard, Steve Garvey, Kevin Mitchell, and Tim Raines. [6]

In the changing political atmosphere of the 1960s, prospective Latino ballplayers, like African-American ones, could fight back against racist insults with much less fear of reprisals. Seeing the righteous anger and early successes of the black power movement, Latinos across the nation began rising up to insist on their rights too: farmworkers in California and Texas; Puerto Rican students joining gang members to create breakfast-for-children programs and public health clinics in major cities (the "Young Lords"); students walking out of public schools to protest inferior education ("blowouts"). [7]

Once again, baseball club owners were reluctant to hire blacks and preferred hiring Latinos. But under the onslaught of the expanding Civil Rights Movement, they had to hire both—especially blacks. In both major leagues Latinos and blacks began winning the majority of Most Valuable Player Awards. The National League, with twice as many blacks and Latinos by 1959 as the American League, won 28 out of 35 All-Star games between 1954 and 1969.

117

The upsurge in social protest movements in the 1960s also emboldened the Players Association, which won a minimum salary hike to $10,000 in 1968 and $40,000 in 1981. As early as 1972, team owners tried to break the union by refusing to pass on some of the money from their new $70 million NBC television contract to the players. The players struck for thirteen days and, the following year, obtained salary arbitration.

By then, the women's movement and the gay rights movement had joined other movements in demanding free choice and equal rights. Baseball players decided the time was ripe to abolish the reserve clause that tied them to their teams, thereby preventing them from choosing freely where to play—"free agency." Armed with court decisions in their favor, the players won the Basic Agreement of 1976, allowing modified free agency applicable to players after six years of big-league play. Average player salaries jumped from $52,300 to $143,756 in 1980 and to about half a million dollars by 1991 and even higher by 1996.[8]

In an effort to eliminate players' free agency, the owners completely stopped their own bidding for free agents for three years in the mid-1980s. Free agent players had no choice but to stay put at whatever salary was offered them. Average player salaries actually declined in 1987. In effect, this secretive owner collusion operated like the old reserve clause. When the Players Association protested, arbitrators penalized the owners some $280 million in damages caused by their illegal collusion.[9]

Former Players Association representative Marvin Miller claimed that the collusion scandal dwarfed the "Black Sox" scandal, when eight Chicago White Sox players took money from gamblers to throw the 1919 World Series. This time, the "fix" involved all the top officials of major-league baseball, including "two baseball commissioners *over three seasons* ... tantamount to fixing, not just games, but entire pennant races, including post-season series."[10]

By the early 1970s, African Americans substantially

outnumbered Latinos in the major leagues. Together, non-whites accounted for 42 percent of all at bats, compared with only 12 percent in the 1950s.[11] Latinos of all "hues" accounted for more than a tenth of major leaguers. The color line lay in tatters, even though racism and anti-Semitism continued in more subtle ways.

As early as 1962 the World Series featured a heavily Latino team, the San Francisco Giants. The Giants had twice as many blacks and Latinos as all of the other National League teams *combined*. They came within a whisker of dethroning the defending World Champion New York Yankees, who themselves had two Latino players.

Sportswriters called the arrival of more and more stars from Latin America an "invasion," as if baseball were a uniquely U.S. sport being intruded upon by outsiders. The truth, of course, was that baseball in Latin America had been intertwined with U.S. baseball since the days the first major-league games were played.

Throughout the late nineteenth century and all of the twentieth century, Latinos and African Americans revolutionized baseball in several areas: hitting, fielding, and speed on the base paths (Bert Campaneris, Roberto Clemente, Rod Carew, Lou Brock, Rickey Henderson, Kenny Lofton); power at the plate (Willie Mays, Hank Aaron, José Canseco, Juan González); and pitching (Rube Foster, Martín Dihigo, the Tiants, Bob Gibson, Juan Marichal, Fernando Valenzuela, Dennis Martínez).

Latinos and African Americans made base-running and fielding strategies more important factors in the game. They captured eighty-nine of ninety-eight league titles for stolen bases from 1947 to 1991 and countless Gold Glove Awards.

Latinos also maintained their tradition of "doing it all." For example, in 1965, Cuban Bert Campaneris, following in his countryman Martín Dihigo's footsteps (see chapter 3), became the first major leaguer ever to play all nine positions in the same game. Venezuelan César Tóvar duplicated the feat three years later, and no one has matched it since. In 1988, Havana-born José Canseco became the first player in history to combine 40 home runs and 40 stolen bases in one season. The press immediately accused the muscular Canseco of using steroids, a charge he flatly denied. Reporters began using the phrase "Canseco shake" to refer to the use of steroids in baseball, even though there was not a shred of evidence to support the original charge.

Starting with Roberto Clemente, Latinos zeroed in on league batting titles. By 1966 four of the top five hitters in the National League were Latinos, with the brothers Mateo "Matty" Alou and Felipe Alou of the Dominican Republic finishing first and second. Felipe's son Moisés is the Montreal batting sensation of the 1990s, with a career average of .301 through 1994. Latinos garnered 9 out of 20 major-league batting titles during the 1960s. Panamanian Rod Carew practically owned the top hitter spot in the 1970s.

Latinos in general, like African Americans, had higher batting and slugging averages than white players. Nonwhites led the National League in home runs for 13 straight years.[12] Most Latino players accomplished all this while playing two seasons, because their fans "back home" still expected them to play in the winter leagues.

Initially, Cuba accounted for the largest number of new Latino major leaguers. By the early 1960s, Cubans Tony Oliva of the Twins, Zoilo Versalles and Tony Perez of the Reds, Luis Tiant, Jr., of the Red Sox, Mike Cuellar of the Orioles, and Bert Campaneris of the Oakland A's "won virtually every offensive and defensive award available to major-league players—Rookie of the Year, Gold Glove, Batting Champion, MVP, and the Cy Young Award."[13]

Then, after the United States broke with the revolutionary government of Fidel Castro in 1960–1961 (see chapter 7), the supply of Cuban ballplayers dried up. Players from other Latin American countries took over, with the

Dominican Republic and Puerto Rico replacing Cuba as the largest source of talent. Venezuela was not far behind, contributing Hall-of-Fame shortstop Luis Aparicio, Jr., to the game.

Aparicio was born in 1934 in Maracaibo, Venezuela, site of one of the world's largest oil reserves. His father, Luis Aparicio, Sr., was a famous all-star shortstop in the Venezuelan leagues who had rejected a contract offer from the Washington Senators in 1939. White Sox general manager Frank Lane outbid Cleveland's Hank Greenberg for Aparicio's services, and by 1956 Luis was Chicago's starting shortstop. At season's end he was Rookie of the Year. The "Go-Go" Sox, under manager Al López, raced to the pennant in 1959, as Luis stole 56 bases. From 1956 through 1964, Luis led the American League in stolen bases. In his eighteen-year major-league career, Luis Aparicio played more games at shortstop than any other player in history and won eight Gold Gloves for fielding. He set the major-league record for double plays, participating in 1,553 of them. He ended his last season with a respectable .273 batting average (lifetime, .262).

Latinos like Aparicio made fielding a science. They also made hitting a science, and some, like Rod Carew and Californian Keith Hernandez, wrote best-selling books on how to hit. Carew and Roberto Clemente were arguably the best and most consistent hitters of the second half of the twentieth century. Carew batted over .300 in 15 consecutive seasons. He set a league batting record of .388 in 1977, winning the batting championship by fifty points, the largest margin in major-league history. He was voted MVP that year. He ended a 19-year career in 1985 with a .328 lifetime average, 3,053 hits, and seven batting titles (only Ty Cobb and Honus Wagner won more). In 1991, Rod Carew became one of only twenty-two players ever to be elected to the Hall of Fame in their first year of eligibility. Like the other great Latino hitter to reach the 3,000-hit mark, Clemente, Carew was a humanitarian. In 1977 he was honored with the Roberto Clemente Award for his charitable work.

Unlike Clemente, in his childhood Carew had no playing fields to hit and run in. As a teenager in the 1950s, Rod and his mother left their home in a crowded all-black neighborhood in the Panama Canal Zone and headed for the concrete jungles and garbage-littered streets of New York City. Young Rod found it difficult to adjust. "The whole transition was tough," he later recalled, "everything from the language to the overcrowding to the rats."[14]

Most of all, U.S.-style racism bothered him, as it did throughout his life. To escape, he played sandlot ball. One day, during a sandlot game, one of Rod's teammates, a Jewish teenager whose father was a Minnesota Twins scout, noticed his abilities and convinced his father to arrange a secret tryout during batting practice before a Yankees-Twins game at Yankee Stadium. When Carew stroked several pitches over the outfield fences, Twins manager Sam Mele shouted, "Get him out of here before somebody sees the kid!"[15] The Twins let him graduate from high school and then signed him up for a $5,000 bonus.

After three years in the minors, Carew moved up to the Twins in 1967, where he played second and first base and was named Rookie of the Year. Twins manager Billy Martin, the onetime second baseman great of the New York Yankees, took Carew under his wing and became "my teacher ... like a second father to me."[16] One thing Carew learned from Martin was how to steal bases. In 1969 he tied Pete Reiser's major-league record for thefts of home (7).

The following year, Rod fell in love with and married Marilynn Levy. Marilynn later recalled what happened when she first brought Rod Carew to her parents' home. It was Passover.

> *My little nieces put up a sign on the wall at the seder, "Guess Who's Coming to Dinner?" It was a popular Sidney Poitier movie of the time about mixed marriages. I took my mother to see it to prepare her.*[17]

Panama native Rod Carew raps out another hit for the Minnesota Twins. The lifetime .328 hitter followed Clemente into the 3,000-hit club and into the Hall of Fame.

In 1979 Carew complained when Twins owner Calvin Griffith made remarks about black fans that Carew viewed as racist. He forced a trade that year and played out his career for the California Angels.

The year he retired from playing baseball, 1985, Carew received the one recognition he cherished above all else: a Medal of Honor from the Panama government and the permanent retirement of his number, 29, in his home country. "It was a heartwarming experience for someone who has purposely kept his Panamanian citizenship in hopes of giving the youth of that country a role model."[18]

Latinos revolutionized hitting and contributed to the improvement in pitching styles taking place in the 1960s. It was a time when the great Jewish southpaw Sandy Koufax and outstanding right-handed fastballers Don Drysdale and Bob Gibson were being compared with the greatest pitchers of all time. The press at first was slow to recognize another great pitcher, a young Latino hurler with an unbelievably high kick before releasing the pitch. Gibson, an African American, acknowledged that this sensational Latino was without doubt "the best pitcher" of the time.[19] Some old-timers said the Latino was the greatest they had ever seen, better even than the fabulous Martín Dihigo or Carl Hubbell. The Latino was none other than future Hall-of-Famer Juan Marichal of the Dominican Republic. Unfortunately, a controversial baseball brawl in late August of 1965 soiled Marichal's reputation and delayed his admission to the Hall of Fame until 1983. But there is much more to say about this extraordinary player.

Juan Antonio Marichal Sánchez (the final name is that

Juan Marichal of the Dominican Republic displays his unique high-kick delivery. The Hall-of-Famer won 243 major-league games, the most ever by a Latino pitcher.

of his mother, according to Latin American custom) was born in 1938 on a farm near the Dominican-Haitian border. When he was only three, Juan's father died and his hard-working mother raised him and his two older brothers and one older sister on the family farm, growing vegetables and tending a herd of goats. Juan's mom wanted him to finish school, but Juan had other ideas. He grew up listening to Dominican baseball games on the radio. "I used to love baseball and dream of playing it. And I will tell you, I feel very proud that, coming from that little community, I went all the way to Cooperstown."[20]

Like other future Dominican stars, little Juan made bats by cutting branches from the *vasima* tree ("like an apple tree, only bigger"), drying them in the sun, trimming and smoothing them. For a glove, he "took a piece of burlap, framed it around a sheet of cardboard, sewed up the sides with fishing line, and bent the whole thing in the middle." For a ball, Juan would take an old golf ball and wrap it in strands of a woman's stocking. Then he took "fifty cents and went to a shoemaker and gave it to him to sew a leather cover onto the ball." If he didn't have the fifty cents, he'd use friction tape instead.

In his early teens, Juan was recruited by the Boston-based United Fruit Company to pitch for its Manzanillo team for $18 a week. In 1956, at age seventeen, after a victory over the Air Force team, Juan received a telegram from the son of the dictator (1930–61) Rafael Trujillo commanding him to "Report to Air Force Right Away." No one dared say no to the dictator in those days.

Trujillo was a former sugar plantation guard trained by the U.S. military as part of a new army created during the Marine occupation of the Dominican Republic in the early 1920s. One of Trujillo's first acts after he became dictator in 1930 was to change the name of the perennial championship contender Sandino baseball team in the northern city of Santiago. The players and fans had given the team its name in the late 1920s. It was named after Augusto César

Sandino, the popular leader of guerrillas then fighting the U.S. Marines in Nicaragua. Many Dominican parents ever since have named their newborn sons César (after Sandino), including a surprising number of major leaguers—César Cedeño, Julio César Franco, etc. The Sandino team's new name became Las Aguilas, the Eagles, a name U.S. diplomats assumed referred to America's national bird. Dominican fans snickered. Their team's name still honored Sandino, known throughout Latin America as "the Eagle of El Chipote" (Sandino's mountain stronghold in Nicaragua).

When workers' revolts threatened, Trujillo killed. In 1937, for example, he ordered the army to slaughter 25,000 Haitian cane cutters who had set up squatters' hovels in the western border provinces not far from Juan Marichal's hometown. To improve his image after this episode, in 1950 Trujillo created a summer league out of four teams that had been playing for decades. One, Escogido, was owned by Trujillo's brother-in-law. Naturally, it soon sported the best players, including Marichal and future major leaguers Felipe, Matty, and Jesús Alou, as well as Ozzie Virgil, the first nonwhite player to join the Detroit Tigers (1958).

After joining the Air Force team, Marichal quickly learned that not only was he not allowed to say no to the dictator but he had better not lose games! He and his teammates were thrown in jail for five days and fined $2 each for losing a doubleheader. Most of the time the team won, led by future major-league stars like Juan and slick-hitting outfielders Manuel "Manny" Jiménez and Manuel "Manny" Mota. Mota compiled a .304 lifetime batting average in 20 major-league seasons.

In his first inning tossing against major leaguers who were playing winter ball in the Dominican Republic in 1957, Juan Marichal threw sidearm and struck out the side. San Francisco Giants coach Salty Parker signed him up for a mere $500 to play on a farm team in Indiana. From there he was moved up to the Giants' AA farm team in Springfield,

Massachusetts, where manager Andy Gilbert taught him how to throw overhand. Marichal became famed for his high kick, which added speed to the fastball and befuddled the batter. In July 1960, Juan Marichal debuted for the Giants by retiring every Philadelphia Phillie batter in order for 6⅓ innings and keeping a no-hitter going until the eighth inning. He finished up the season with a sterling 6–2 record.

That September Juan took a room in a house near Candlestick Park owned by Blanche Laverne "Mama" Johnson, a friendly African American. Fellow Giant Felipe Alou and his wife, María, lived nearby. Felipe's younger brother and Giants teammate, Matty Alou, also moved into Johnson's home.

Dominican outfielder Felipe Rojas Alou, whose youth had been similar to Marichal's, had preceded Juan to the majors in 1958. He compiled a .286 lifetime average in 17 seasons. He later managed teams in the Dominican Republic and Venezuela. In 1994 he was the only Latino team manager in the majors. That year, after leading the Montreal Expos to a 74–40 record in a strike-shortened season, he received 27 of the 28 first-place votes for Manager of the Year honors.

Felipe Alou first became a baseball fanatic after Jackie Robinson's 1948 spring-training season in the Dominican Republic (see chapter 4). In 1955, at age nineteen, Felipe went to the Pan American Games in Mexico City as a track and field runner and javelin thrower. When the baseball team needed an extra player he picked up the bat and slugged some long homers. Major-league scouts took one look and said, "We must have him."[21]

Alou signed on with the San Francisco Giants, even though he wished to remain home. But an uncle had criticized the dictator Trujillo, Alou's father had lost his job, and Felipe had been forced to drop out of the University of Santo Domingo, where he had begun studying in a pre-med program. "As I looked at the tired walls of our home, at the crowded rooms, at the weariness in my parents' faces

—all accentuated by our crude, flickering little lamp—I could only hope that better days were coming and that I would help bring them."

Felipe and his brothers did indeed bring "better days." Felipe's hitting was excelled by that of his brother Matty (lifetime average of .307), although no Dominican could match Felipe's home-run power in those days. Felipe hit 207 homers in his major-league career. Later, Dominican sluggers George Bell, Pedro Guerrero, and Rico Carty passed the 200 homer mark. Youngest brother Jesús Alou batted .280 lifetime. The three Alous' combined 5,000 hits surpassed the previous record set by the three brothers of the DiMaggio family.

In 1961 the Dominican people were growing restless under the iron heel of Trujillo's tyranny. The CIA ordered Trujillo assassinated, and Dominicans celebrated in the streets. U.S. baseball scouts celebrated too. Pittsburgh scout Howie Haak remembered that he had been told "you'll never sign anyone who Trujillo wants playing for [his team].... It wasn't until we [the CIA] got rid of him that the doors were opened."[22]

Juan Marichal waited for political matters to calm down and then married Alma Rosa, on March 28, 1962. When fans later saw him at the American Embassy seeking residence papers for himself and his new wife, they mistakenly thought he was becoming a citizen of the country that had backed Trujillo's dictatorship for so many decades. This made Juan extremely nervous.

In 1962 the three Alou brothers, Orlando Cepeda, shortstop José Pagán, and Juan Marichal led the San Francisco Giants to their first pennant. Five of the nine players fielded by the Giants in their pennant-clinching win against the Los Angeles Dodgers were Latinos.

The people of the Dominican Republic finally realized Marichal had not taken out U.S. citizenship papers. They gave him and the Alous a rousing welcome home at the Santo Domingo airport. Thousands arrived by bus and by donkey from outlying towns and villages to cheer the first Dominicans ever to play in a World Series.

Despite injuries, Marichal had finished 13–10 in 1961 and achieved an 18–11 record in 1962. In the 1963 season, when he won 25 games and lost only 8, he threw a no-hitter against the Houston Colt 45s. For the ninth inning of that game he did what he always did when winning. He literally ran out to the mound and almost without pause struck out two batters and got the third on a foul pop fly. Marichal's exuberant pitching style made him extremely popular. Juan was even more proud of a subsequent 4-hour, 10-minute, 16-inning pitching duel that he won against Milwaukee Braves ace southpaw Warren Spahn, thanks to a Willie Mays home run. Giants manager Alvin Dark called it "the greatest pitched game I ever saw."[23]

In 1964, Dark, a white Southerner, fielded a team of mostly nonwhite starters: three Latinos and three African Americans. In late July, Dark was quoted by *Newsday* as saying:

> *We have trouble because we have so many Spanish-speaking and Negro players on our team. They are just not able to perform up to the white ball player when it comes to mental alertness.... You can't make most Negro and Spanish players have the pride in their team that you can get from white players. And they just aren't as sharp mentally. They aren't able to adjust to situations because they don't have that mental alertness.[24]*

In his autobiography, Marichal told of incidents where Dark called the Latinos "boys" and kicked Latino players' food off the table after a losing game. Giants first baseman Orlando Cepeda later wrote in his autobiography:

> *I can easily and honestly say that Alvin Dark was a liar and a bigot.... he hated all the black and Latin players, and he divided the team into three camps: the*

blacks, the whites, and the Latins.... I'll say this much
for Dark. I don't think he's the only one in baseball
who thinks that way. [25]

Cepeda remembered that when he reported to spring training in 1962 he saw a sign that said "Speak English, You're in America." Dark told the players to "stop speaking Spanish in the clubhouse." Cepeda informed Dark:

It's my language, and this is a crime against my
heritage and my roots. When American players come
to Puerto Rico in the winter they don't speak Spanish,
and it doesn't bother me at all. [26]

Because Cepeda was a large, proud, and muscular black Latino, fans affectionately called him "the Baby Bull." Cepeda, with a lifetime average of .297 and 379 home runs, in 1967 was the first of only three players ever to be voted unanimously National League Most Valuable Player (the others being Mike Schmidt, 1980, and Jeff Bagwell, 1994). He was the son of the famed Puerto Rican baseball superstar Pedro "Perucho" ["Pete"] Cepeda, also known as "the Puerto Rican Babe Ruth."

Orlando Cepeda started his major-league career in 1958, the year the Giants moved from New York to San Francisco, by stroking a towering home run off Don Drysdale in his second at bat. Named Rookie of the Year, he belted an average of 34 home runs a year in his first 7 seasons, hitting well over .300 in 6 of them. [27]

To cool the racial fires, Giants management replaced Alvin Dark for the 1965 season with Herman Franks, who spoke Spanish from the days when he used to manage winter ball in Puerto Rico. Latino players welcomed the managerial change, of course. Marichal, however, was grumbling. After a 21–8 season in 1964, he received a paltry pay hike to $60,000 for 1965 while his white rivals Drysdale and Koufax were pulling down well over $100,000.

Other events in 1965 added special tensions to U.S.

*Puerto Rican first baseman Orlando Cepeda
was named Rookie of the Year in 1958.*

baseball. "Riots" by angry young ghetto blacks were becoming commonplace. Additional new civil rights legislation was being debated in the U.S. Congress. At the same time, the war in Vietnam was heating up. The United States was getting bogged down in its longest and most costly war, finally losing it in 1975. Black athletes were speaking out. Said the great heavyweight boxing champion Muhammad Ali: "No Vietnamese ever called me Nigger."[28]

Just as bad, so far as many Latino ballplayers were concerned, the United States invaded the Dominican Republic to quash a people's uprising that sought to restore to the presidency Juan Bosch, the democratically elected president earlier overthrown by the U.S.-backed Dominican Armed Forces. The U.S. government saw agrarian reformer Bosch as a threat to the interests of major U.S. sugar companies. Throughout most of the summer of 1965, darker-skinned Dominicans backing Bosch were engaged in street fighting against U.S. marines.

Dominican ballplayers like Marichal worried about their loved ones back home. "What I yearned for most of all," Juan later wrote, "was a stable, democratic form of government."[29] Tens of thousands of U.S. troops finally "restored order" in Santo Domingo but not completely. The Dominican winter baseball league season had to be canceled. The following spring Marichal ran a full-page ad in Santo Domingo's most widely read newspaper, urging Dominicans to vote in the presidential elections. Voters reportedly quipped that if Marichal were running for president "it would be a landslide."

In fact, the winning candidate, Joaquín Balaguer, former secretary for the late dictator Rafael Trujillo, picked as his running mate Marichal's cousin, also named Juan Marichal. The shrewd winner, Balaguer, who in the mid-1990s was still president (even though old and blind), called himself "the Marichal of the Presidential Palace."[30]

While the 1965 shooting was still going on in the streets of Santo Domingo, a nasty fight between Juan Marichal

and Los Angeles Dodgers catcher Johnny Roseboro erupted at Candlestick Park. Perhaps because the two combatants were Latino and African American, the white baseball press played up the skirmish way out of proportion. There have been far worse fights in baseball history before and since.[31]

The incident occurred at a Dodgers-Giants game during the teams' by then traditional late-season pennant race. The Giants-Dodgers rivalry, constantly hyped by the press, dated back to the days when the teams had played in New York and Brooklyn, respectively. Now it was being further fueled by the racial tensions wracking the nation. Early in the four-game series Don Drysdale came close to beaning the Giants all-star center fielder, African-American Willie Mays, with two brush-back pitches.

In the final game, Marichal decked two Dodger hitters in the second inning. One of them, African-American Maurie Wills, was the team leader and roommate of catcher Johnny Roseboro. Next time Mays came to bat, Dodger ace Sandy Koufax tried to deck him, but the ball went sailing over Mays's head all the way to the backstop. According to Roseboro, the gentle mannered Koufax was:

> *constitutionally incapable of throwing at anyone's*
> *head, so I decided to take matters into my own hands.*
> *When Juan came up, I went out to tell Sandy to pitch*
> *him low and inside and I'd buzz Marichal from*
> *behind the plate.*[32]

Then, when Marichal strode up to the plate to take his turn at bat, he dug in, determined to defend his reputation as baseball's best-hitting pitcher.[33] Just as Roseboro

Anti-American slogans greet U.S.
soldiers in the city of Santo Domingo,
following a U.S. invasion of the
Dominican Republic in 1965.

had instructed, Koufax fired a low-inside pitch. Roseboro caught, then dropped the ball. Scooping it up with his bare hand, he zipped it back to Koufax—by way of Marichal's head. "I guess Juan's Latin blood began to boil," Roseboro later cracked.[34]

Marichal felt Roseboro's "buzz" ball, as it is known in the trade, nick his ear. He shouted at Roseboro, "Why did you do that?" According to Marichal, Roseboro answered "F—— you!"[35] Marichal swung his bat and caught Roseboro on the side of the face. Instantly, both teams' benches cleared and a brief brawl ensued.

According to Roseboro, "I had provoked [the incident]... I saw it [the ball] go by his nose. It was intentional all right. I meant for him to feel it."[36]

Mays went on to win the game for the Giants with a three-run homer. Afterwards, Marichal made a public apology, but league president Giles suspended him for eight playing days and fined him $1,750, "the highest," according to Roseboro, "ever handed a big leaguer."[37] Marichal was also prohibited from pitching in an upcoming series in Los Angeles, in his view "because of the recency of the Watts riots." He was referring to the uprising in the black neighborhood of Watts in Los Angeles, triggered by acts of police brutality. With feelings running so high, Juan figured organized baseball did not want "to complicate [things] by having me appear on the field there." His eight-day suspension became "eleven days on account of my being barred from L.A."[38]

In the eyes of most observers, this cost the Giants the 1965 pennant. Wrote Roseboro:

> Of course, we wanted one of the best pitchers in the game out of our pennant fight. As it was, he missed two starts and we won the pennant by two games.... Marichal was famous and he helped make Roseboro famous. He was a villain and I was a hero. No action was taken against me.[39]

Roseboro sued Marichal for more than $100,000 and settled out of court seven years later for around $7,000.

After the Roseboro-Marichal confrontation of August 1965, the press had a field day portraying Marichal as a "hot-tempered Latino." Latino players in general became more stereotyped than ever as out-of-control athletes who did not play "by the rules." Yet prior to the incident, the baseball world had nicknamed Juan Marichal the "Laughing Boy" because of his "ever-present grin and sunny disposition."[40]

Juan Marichal told baseball commentator Rob Ruck in the 1980s, when Latinos were still being stereotyped as "too emotional," that "there are a lot of American players that do the same. It's part of the game. It's excitement that makes you act like that." But the press still portrays Latinos as "hot-tempered" today. What if all white ballplayers were negatively stereotyped as a bunch of cheats and frauds, as shown by the gambling and even criminal behavior of players during the Black Sox scandal or Pete Rose's fall from grace?

For 1966, after Marichal's third straight 20-win season and an unbelievable ERA of 2.13, the Giants offered Marichal no salary hike at all. Juan held out and received $75,000. In 1967, after a blistering 25–6 season with a 2.23 ERA that earned him a picture on the cover of *Time* magazine, Juan held out again and finally got the six-figure sum he wanted: $100,000.

The Giants pressured Marichal and the other Latino players not to play winter ball in the Dominican Republic, an unthinkable thing for Juan, who observed, "If you don't play, the whole country gets on you."[41] Team owners also accused Marichal of exaggerating or even faking his injuries. A 1962 foot fracture did not show up on the first X rays. Not until four years later did a fresh X ray of the increasingly deformed foot show the original fracture. When Marichal then asked the doctor to X ray his other foot, the good one, the doctor refused:

It will turn out you have won ninety games on two broken feet, and I do not wish to have to be the doctor to say this in a report, because they will make me out to be a publicity-seeker. [42]

On the eve of the 1983 Hall of Fame vote, Johnny Roseboro publicly called for Marichal's election, urging everyone to forget about the 1965 incident. Marichal's amazing lifetime record showed 243 wins and only 142 losses; a spectacularly low ERA of 2.89; six 20-win seasons; 52 shutouts; one no-hitter; and eight times an All-Star (winning two of the games). Marichal received 83.6 percent of the votes cast. He dedicated his final triumph to the Dominican people and all Latinos. Back home, Dominicans danced in the streets.

By then, Marichal had retired to the Dominican Republic with the nickname of "El Millonario" ("the Millionaire"). He later became director of Latin American scouting in his homeland for the Oakland A's.

7

siete

"NO STEALING

IN THIS

REVOLUTION!"

There's no stealing here anymore, not even in baseball.
> — Said in jest by Cuban premier Fidel Castro[1]

The only way we want to compete with the United States is through baseball. If the U.S. presence has left us something beautiful, it's baseball.
> — Humberto Ortega, Nicaraguan minister of defense[2]

In 1959, on the newly proclaimed national holiday of July 26, Cuban baseball fans were attending a game between their famous Havana Sugar Kings and the Rochester Red Wings. An air of excitement filled the ballpark. The Sugar Kings had been playing championship-quality ball for thirteen years and now wanted to win the triple A International League (IL) title for the Cuban Revolution that had started exactly six years earlier and catapulted Fidel Castro to power in January 1959.[3]

During a promotional two-inning contest two days before the holiday game, Castro pitched one of the innings for the Army team, the "Barbudos" ("Bearded Rebels"), against the Military Police team. He fanned two, the second on a pitch too high and inside to be in the strike zone. A happy Castro trotted to home plate to shake the hand of the umpire, as fans laughed their approval.

One story making the rounds was that once when Castro was on the mound a player stole second base on him. "El comandante" sternly waved the speedster back to first, wagging his finger and proclaiming: "No stealing in this Revolution!"

A still more famous tale is that the Revolution's bearded leader had once, in earlier days, tried out for the Washington Senators. Researchers claim that the Senators' top scout, Joe Cambria, recruited Castro with an offer of $5,000. Castro turned down the offer, apparently preferring to continue his college education. Later he claimed that he was "a mediocre pitcher—dangerous only because his pitch might have hit someone."[4]

As the cliffhanger holiday game went into extra innings, sounds like firecrackers came from the stands. Overly zealous fans were celebrating the July 26 anniversary of the start of the Revolution by wildly shooting off their guns. One bullet grazed the cap of Red Wing third-base coach Frank Verdi. Fortunately, Verdi's cap had a metal helmet liner. Another bullet grazed twenty-one-year-old Havana shortstop Leo "Chico" Cárdenas, later to become famous in the U.S. major leagues playing nearly 2,000 games. The game had to be called.

Cuba's sports director promptly cabled an apology to the Red Wings for the incident, downplayed by much of the sporting press in both countries. Rochester general manager George Sisler, however, vowed he would not allow his team ever again to play in Cuba. Sugar Kings owner Bobby Maduro, later to become a chief assistant to the U.S. commissioner of baseball, complained:

> *How can Sisler or anybody else so misconstrue a show like we are having here; it's like the Fourth of July in the States. You can't control things like this. Rochester's refusal to play today will damage baseball in Cuba, in our league, and baseball everywhere.* [5]

At the time Sisler and Maduro were quarreling, the Cold War between the Soviet Union and the United States was heating up. The U.S. government was quick to see "communists" behind any serious attempts at reform in Latin America, including the Cuban Revolution's agrarian and housing reforms and its efforts to ban racial segregation in public facilities. Despite Sisler's grumbling, the top IL brass decided to complete the 1959 season schedule. The Sugar Kings went on to win the IL pennant and the Junior World Series in Havana. The championship team included future major-league stars Chico Cárdenas, Octavio "Cookie" Rojas, and Puerto Rican relief pitcher Luis Arroyo.

In 1960, after Texaco and Esso (today's Exxon) refused to refine the oil Cuba's government had been importing from the Soviet Union since the early 1950s, Castro nationalized the big U.S. oil firms and several other large corporations, assuring them they would be compensated. The U.S. government severed diplomatic relations, prohibited Americans from traveling to Cuba, and slapped an economic embargo on the island that would last for more than three decades.

The IL promptly moved the Sugar Kings to Jersey City, New Jersey. Castro denounced the move as an act of aggression. At the same time, the U.S. Congress defeated a bill that would have put baseball under the government's antitrust laws. The owners were still free to do what they wished.

Most U.S. sportswriters blamed Castro's nationalizations of U.S. businesses for the "end to the golden age of baseball in Cuba."[6] U.S. bombs did not help matters. In early 1961, following U.S. air strikes on Havana that destroyed the Cuban Air Force and some nearby suburban homes, a U.S.-trained military force of Cuban exiles landed on Cuba's Playa Girón ("Bay of Pigs") to "liberate" the island. The invasion failed miserably. Almost all the Cuban people rose up to defend their nation's honor against "*Yanqui* imperialism." President John F. Kennedy took full responsibility for the invasion.

During the years leading up to the Cuban Revolution, more than a hundred Cuban players, including many former Sugar Kings, graced the U.S. major leagues. Some thirty of them played before U.S. baseball was officially desegregated, and ninety played after that. Almost all played or arrived before the 1960 imposition of the U.S. economic embargo. Their names read like a Who's Who in post-1950s baseball: polished hurlers Mike Cuellar, Camilo Pascual, and Luis Tiant, Jr.; Minnesota's batting champion Tony Oliva; Cincinnati's slugging first baseman Tony Pérez;

In April 1960, Cuban premier Fidel Castro throws out the ceremonial first ball of an International League game played between the Havana Sugar Kings and the Rochester Red Wings. Baseball and politics have often been intertwined in Cuba and other Latin American countries, just as they have in the United States.

Brooklyn outfielder Sandy Amoros; major-league stolen-base king Bert Campaneris; and steady-hitting slick infielders like Rigoberto "Tito" Fuentes, Cookie Rojas, and Tony Taylor.

Tony Pérez whacked 379 home runs and drove in 1,652 runs during his 23-year career that ended in 1986 (lifetime batting average .279). Right-handed pitcher Camilo Pascual, who started out with the Washington Senators in 1954 and was nicknamed "Little Potato," retired in 1971 with a lifetime ERA of 3.63. Mike Cuellar (lifetime ERA, 3.14) was considered by many to be the major-leagues' best left-handed pitcher in the early 1970s.[7]

Tony Oliva was the last Cuban signed by Joe Cambria. Oliva left Cuba only days before the Bay of Pigs invasion. Playing outfield for the Minnesota Twins in 1964, Tony became the first American League rookie to win a batting championship (.323). Hobbled by injuries, he went on to compile a .304 lifetime average with 220 home runs.

Dagberto Blanco Campaneris, son of a Matanzas rope factory worker, was in Costa Rica for an amateur tournament when the Bay of Pigs invasion occurred. At the tournament a scout for the Kansas City A's signed him and his teammate Tito Fuentes. In an effort to raise attendance, the lowly A's let Campaneris play all nine positions in a 1965 game.

Known as "Bert" and "Campy," Campaneris soon began lifting the A's out of the cellar, especially after the A's moved to Oakland. There, during the early 1970s, manager Dick Williams catered to the Bay Area's Latino and black empowerment movements by allowing his Latino players to speak Spanish and sport mustaches and his black players to have Afros. Fans loved it. The players responded with 101 victories and a division title in 1971. The following three seasons, the A's swept the World Series, establishing the longest reign as World Champions since the New York Yankees of the early 1950s.

The 1973 World Series MVP was Oakland's Reggie

*Cuban-born Bert Campaneris shows off the
equipment he used when playing all nine positions
in a 1965 game for the Kansas City A's.*

Jackson, known as Mr. October for his hot hitting in the autumn classic. Jackson was a hero for many African Americans. Few baseball fans realized that his mother was a Latina and his full name was Reginal Martínez Jackson. Reggie readily acknowledged that "Campy" should have won the MVP award. A's owner Charlie O. Finley later confirmed that "it was Campy who made everything go."[8] Campaneris closed out his career in 1983 with 646 stolen bases, ranking him eleventh in baseball history.

In 1957 a Cuban juvenile all-star team member was discouraged by his father from pursuing a career in the U.S. majors. Luis "Lefty" Tiant, Sr., the spitball ace who had long ago outdueled the New York Giant star Carl Hubbell in a Havana exhibition game and played several years for the Negro American League's New York Cubans, explained to his son that "there is no place in the major leagues for a black man."[9] Two years later, young Tiant left Cuba to play ball for the Mexico City Tigers.

In 1961 Luis planned a honeymoon in Cuba with his new wife, Mexican softball player María del Refugio Navarro. His father, knowing that he would not be able to have a paying professional baseball career in his homeland, advised him to stay in Mexico. Tiant did, progressing to greener pastures in *el norte*, where by 1964 he was a U.S. major leaguer. In 1968, imitating some of the tricky body moves of his father, he compiled the best American League ERA since Walter Johnson's back in 1919. Luis Tiant, Jr., went on to have four 20-win seasons, lead the American League in shutouts for three seasons, and chalk up one of the best win-loss records in major-league history (229–172, with 49 shutouts and 2,426 strikeouts over 19 years).

Because of the U.S. embargo and travel bans, Luis Tiant, Jr.'s parents had never seen him pitch in the majors. Then, in 1975, during a diplomatic thaw in U.S.-Cuba relations, Luis's parents were able to come to the United States to watch him play for the Boston Red Sox, the first family reunion in fifteen years. For a game in late August at Fenway

Park, Luis "Lefty" Tiant, Sr., the skinny and gray-haired superstar of the Negro American League, threw out the first ball as the fans broke into applause.

The Red Sox went on to the World Series that year, and sports commentators and TV cameras zeroed in on the Tiant family. A proud papa watched his thirty-five-year-old son win the Series opener on a 5-hit shutout against the power-hitting Cincinnati "Big Red Machine." Tiant went on to win another game in the World Series before the Reds mounted a ninth-inning rally in game seven to edge the Red Sox 4 games to 3. The Fenway faithful fell silent.

During the Tiant family visit as well as on several other occasions, Fidel Castro tried to use "baseball diplomacy" in an effort to mend fences with the U.S. government. In 1977, Castro invited the New York Yankees to play in Havana. Perhaps fearing a Yankees defeat, baseball commissioner Bowie Kuhn discouraged the idea.

Meanwhile, back in Cuba, baseball changed. Athletes played for free, and no admission was charged. The great Negro-league pitching ace Martín Dihigo returned to his homeland to serve as minister of sports and instruct youngsters in baseball. Havana's Gran Stadium was enlarged to seat 55,000 and rebaptized Estadio Latinoamericano. A bust of Dihigo at the stadium was sculpted, calling him simply "El Inmortal" ("the Immortal One").[10] Some nine other stadiums expanded seating capacities to 20,000 or more. Cuban leagues grew larger, too.

At a typical game, sweeping the basepaths were older groundskeepers dressed in work clothes rather than prancing, scantily clad teenage girls. Electric scoreboards flashed batting averages instead of beer commercials. With less drunkenness and rowdiness in the stands, policemen were no longer needed at the games. Fans who won the scramble in the stands to grab a foul ball now returned the precious prize to the field "with a virtuous flourish."[11]

Naturally, Cubans loved their baseball heroes as much as any other group of fans. Superstars were expected to serve as good role models. Popular players formed their own volunteer work brigades to help in the construction of new homes or other urgent tasks of the Revolution. The idea of an athlete advertising a sneaker or a fast-food outlet became foreign to most Cubans.

Article 51 of the new Cuban Constitution stated: "Everyone has the right to physical education, sports and recreation."[12] Voluntary sports councils known as CVDs sprang up—120,000 by 1961. The government created specialized sports schools and provided numerous athletic scholarships for the less well-off.

In Cuba today, baseball diamonds appear in neighborhood after neighborhood. According to Raúl Castro (Fidel's brother):

> *Under capitalism, sport, like almost everything, was an end, and the end was profit. Sport under a socialist regime is a means, before everything else, for the self-improvement of the citizen, for the betterment of his health.*[13]

A well-researched book published by the University of Pittsburgh Press in 1994 concluded that Cuba achieved its goal of "democratization of sports."[14]

A full fifth of the Cuban population participates regularly in sports activities today. More than half a million men actively play organized baseball. At the same time, in international sporting contests Cuba has proven itself one of the world's top ten nations. From 1963 to 1991 the Cuban baseball team won the Pan-American Games every year except for 1987.

After the U.S. economic embargo blocked the shipment of sports equipment, Cuba produced its own gloves, balls, and bats. Today, Cuba exports baseballs and other sporting goods. When the Clinton administration tightened the embargo in the 1990s, the revenues from these exports dropped off. To help economize on the use of electricity,

The Cuban national team (dark uniforms) celebrates after winning the gold medal in the baseball competition at the 1992 Summer Olympics.

night baseball games had to be canceled, a severe blow for sports fans.

In 1992, for the first time ever, the Olympic Games offered a gold medal in baseball. To no one's surprise, the Cubans won it. This triumph brought their record in international baseball competition to an impressive 71–1. The press promptly dubbed the Cuban Olympic baseball team "the other Dream Team" (the more famous one being the U.S. basketball squad). Right to the present, most baseball observers believe that the Cuban National Team can beat any major-league team put up against them.[15]

In 1980, Barbaro Garbey became the first Cuban in almost twenty years to join a major-league club. After he admitted to accepting bribes and fixing games in Cuba, the government banned him from playing ball. Arriving with other Mariel boat refugees, he was recruited by the Detroit Tigers and hit .387 in 196 games as a designated hitter and utility player. But Garbey soon faced trouble in the United States, too. First he was suspended after allegedly striking a fan with a bat, and then he was banished after he was arrested for possession of cocaine. He now plays pro ball in Mexico.

In the 1990s, major-league scouts began visiting Cuba regularly in hopes of luring away Cuban stars. In 1991 René Arocha defected at the Pan American Games in Havana and eventually became a relief pitcher for the St. Louis Cardinals. U.S. baseball owners hope to duplicate with Cubans what their National Hockey League counterparts have achieved with former Soviet hockey players.

But in 1977 the U.S. government had outlawed the entry of Cuban baseball players, and in 1991 it prevented baseball scouts from going to Cuba for the Pan American Games. It even tried banning television coverage of the Pan Am Games, but ABC won a freedom of speech case and televised the event anyway.

Despite Cuba's economic problems, most Cuban players apparently remain appreciative of the chances given them by the Revolution. They earn money at their regular jobs when not playing ball, and they receive some fringe benefits as well as fans' adoration. Players have an unusually close relationship with the fans. As Matanzas right fielder Wilfredo Sánchez jokingly says: "After every game, I have nine and a half million people waiting outside the stadium who want to explain to me, for the good of Cuba, what I did wrong."[16]

Omar Linares, the outstanding third baseman of the Poder Popular (People's Power) team, reportedly turned down a multimillion-yen offer to play in Japan. In 1985 the Toronto Blue Jays recruited him in a way that avoided the difficulty of obtaining a U.S. visa to play major-league ball: Linares would play only home games in Canada! Linares said "no thanks." Linares echoes a widespread patriotic spirit when he says: "We are not going to be overrun by the United States. We prefer to die in our country before we submit."[17]

Miami's large Cuban-American population, also avid baseball players and fans, is sensitive to charges by some Latino fans of playing second-rate, "sub-Cuban" baseball. There are fifteen Cuban-American baseball schools in Miami, including one run by Camilo Pascual's brother Carlos, a scout for the Baltimore Orioles. At least one high school team and one American Legion team in Miami have fielded only Cuban-American players for several years.

Some of the children of Cuban exile families have gone on to become big-league baseball players, including Rafael Palmeiro and Danny Tartabull. The most famous is Havana-born (1964) José Canseco, a slugger who had hit 276 home runs lifetime through 1994, including 31 in the abbreviated 1994 season for the Texas Rangers before he was injured and traded to become the Boston Red Sox designated hitter.

The other modern-day Latin American revolution to "prohibit stealing" occurred in Nicaragua in 1979. It drew a lot of sympathy from U.S. citizens from all walks of life, including baseball players and fans. Rumor had it that the Minnesota Twins' Nicaraguan pitcher Al Williams had spent his off-seasons fighting with the "Sandinista" guerrillas, named after the Nicaraguan patriot Augusto César Sandino, whose guerrilla army drove out the U.S. Marines in the early 1930s.

Perhaps to avoid the total isolation imposed on Cuba, the Nicaraguan Revolution's Sandinista leadership seemed to promise a democratic form of social reforms mixed with capitalism. After the Revolution, they left more than half of the economy in the hands of private owners.

As they watched the ups and downs of their rocky revolution, Nicaraguan baseball fans enthusiastically followed the exploits of their countryman Dennis Martínez, a Montreal Expos pitcher. In 1991 the crafty curveball ace, at age thirty-six, threw a perfect no-hit game, retiring 27 batters in order. It was only the fifteenth time in history anyone had done it. That same year he racked up the National League's most shutouts and complete games and won the ERA title.

In his previous 15 years with Baltimore and Montreal, Martínez had compiled a 163–134 record and established himself as one of baseball's stellar right-handers. In 1980 Martínez returned to revolutionary Nicaragua with a team of Baltimore reservists to play against an all-star team from a newly created national amateur league of ten teams. Fans went wild as the Nicaraguan team won one game and tied the other.

During the 1994–95 baseball strike, Martínez boldly criticized baseball owners. As a free agent, he signed on with the Cleveland Indians in 1994, in a high-paid $9 million two-year deal. Known as "El Presidente," Dennis Martínez is one of six pitchers to win 100 games or more in each major league. He helped anchor the Cleveland pitching staff and pitched well in the 1995 World Series.

In the 1980s and early 1990s, the administrations of presidents Ronald Reagan and George Bush did not look kindly on the young Nicaraguan revolutionaries taking over a country the United States had long dominated. Reagan called them all a bunch of "communists" and mounted a "dirty war" to overthrow their government. Former supporters of Nicaraguan dictator Somoza, calling themselves "Contras," carried out assassinations of schoolteachers, farmers, and other civilians, in a prolonged effort to destroy the reforms of the Revolution. The Reagan administration trained and equipped the Contras and, to head up the project, Reagan assigned a Vietnam War veteran, Lieutenant Colonel Oliver North.[18]

Because so many Americans sympathized with the Sandinista cause and opposed U.S. intervention, the U.S. Congress voted to cut off funds for the Contras. To raise more money for the Contras, North tried to "prove" Cuban influence over the Sandinistas. "He pointed conclusively to the baseball diamonds that were so visible in air reconnaissance photos taken over Nicaragua."[19] North was about a hundred years late in showing Cuban influence though. Baseball had long been Nicaragua's national pastime and was as home-grown as the Sandinistas themselves, most of whom grew up loving baseball.

Despite its tribulations, Nicaragua somehow managed to keep up its baseball teams throughout the long Contra war of the 1980s, which claimed more than 50,000 lives out of a population of 3 million. As in Cuba, baseball was deprofessionalized. There were fewer players, because any young man dreaming of becoming a major leaguer found himself carrying a gun in his hands instead of a bat.

With hunger stalking the land as the result of the prolonged Contra war, President Daniel Ortega lost his bid for reelection in 1990 to a U.S.-financed candidate who had once been a member of the Sandinista government. Many voters said they were tired of the war and hoped that the United States would "lighten up" if the U.S.-preferred candidate won. Many hoped that the day would come again when baseballs could finally replace bullets in their daily lives.

8
ocho

STILL

UNDERPAID—

EXCEPT

FOR A FEW!

It has been suggested that an all-star Dominican team might be able to win the World Series; a San Pedro [de Macorís] team could certainly give most major league teams a run for the pennant."
— Baseball writers John S. Bowman and Joel Zoss[1]

On the edge of town is a big billboard: "Welcome to San Pedro de Macorís. The City Which Has Given the Most Major Leaguers to the World."[2]

Amazingly, this city of 85,000 in the southeastern sugarcane countryside of the Dominican Republic has sent dozens of first-rate shortstops to U.S. baseball. It also has sent sluggers like George Bell, who hit 47 homers and won the MVP award for Toronto in 1987. Other San Pedro sons have included big-name stars like Joaquín Andújar, Rico Carty, César Cedeño, Tony Fernández, Julio César Franco, Alfredo Griffin, Pedro Guerrero, Stan Javier, José Offerman, Rafael Ramírez, Juan Samuel, and Sammy Sosa.

A third of the more than 100 Dominican players to have made it to the majors by 1988 got there via San Pedro. Tony Fernández, who took a 12-year .285 average into the 1995 season as the anchor of the New York Yankees infield grew up there. As a boy, he was hobbled by bone chips in his knee and barely able to run. He idolized slick-fielding All-Star Alfredo Griffin (lifetime batting average .258), the dark-skinned San Pedro shortstop who helped make the Toronto Blue Jays a contender from 1979 to 1985. After an operation on his knee at age fifteen, Tony went on to take Griffin's job and become an All-Star American League shortstop himself.

Several San Pedro youths have gone from rags to riches. Rico Carty, César Cedeño, and Pedro Guerrero, for example, all signed bonuses for $3,000 or less. Their skills eventually earned them much more, inspiring other Dominicans to choose baseball careers as an escape route from poverty in a land known for its high unemployment.

Not far from San Pedro de Macorís, the U.S. corporation Gulf & Western (G&W) took over the La Romana sugar industry complex after the 1965 U.S. invasion and ran it, according to several human rights reports, like a prison labor camp. Visiting U.S. labor union delegations were not allowed inside to examine work conditions. Like Trujillo, G&W encouraged baseball.[3]

Slugger Sammy Sosa smacks one of his 36 homers in the 1995 season. A remarkable number of major leaguers, including Sosa, have come from the Dominican city of San Pedro de Macorís.

Outfielder Rico Carty was born in 1941 in nearby Consuelo, where workers cut the cane for the San Pedro mills. When Rico Carty was only five years old, a hard-fought strike won a shorter workday for sugarcane workers. After the strike Trujillo repressed political organizing more severely than ever. Rico's father, a sugar mill worker, supported an Irish priest from Canada who was organizing townspeople against Trujillo's repression. He and the priest helped bring the West Indian and Dominican communities together around the game of baseball in the late 1940s and 1950s. Rico's dad went on to manage the Consuelo team that won the 1957 amateur championship.

As a teenager, Rico grew to a height of 6 feet 3 inches. Cutting logs at the mill one day, he complained to his uncle: "This is for animals, it's not for me."[4] He turned his full attention to baseball, playing for his father's team and blossoming into a teenage slugger. In the late 1950s he became a star for Escogido, the team owned by Trujillo's brother-in-law. At the 1959 Pan American Games in Chicago, U.S. major-league scouts rushed up to Rico with batches of contracts in their hands. Barely understanding English, Rico signed each contract—nine of them. But he took no bonuses. Trujillo's agents took Rico Carty to court to force him to stay on the Escogido team. Then George Trautman, head of the U.S. minor leagues, persuaded Dominican officials that Rico was innocent because he had not accepted any bonuses when he signed.

In 1964, with Trujillo no longer around to stop him, Rico broke into the majors with a bang, playing for the Milwaukee Braves. He batted .330 with 22 home runs and 88 RBIs. By 1970 he was National League batting champion, hitting a fantastic .366, the best since Stan Musial's .376 in 1948. When Carty's name was left off the All-Star Game ballot, he became the first starting player ever to be elected by write-in votes.

Carty contracted tuberculosis in 1969, undermining his attractiveness to big-league clubs. In 1973 he was traded three times and even did a stint in the Mexican League. But despite playing out his career with repeated injuries, Carty retired at the end of the 1979 season with a .299 lifetime average. He took up coaching in the Dominican Republic after that.

Despite his impressive career, the press often labeled Rico Carty, and any other Latino who ever showed anger on the field, "a typical Latino hothead," while celebrating whites like famed player and manager Billy Martin who regularly threw temper tantrums.

Another player that the press initially lambasted was San Pedro's Julio César Franco. Franco took a career average of .301 into the 1995 season. Before his trade to the Texas Rangers, the Cleveland media gave him a hard time. Yet in Texas he gained the reputation of being a good team player and a positive influence on younger Latino players.

Another San Pedro player who "made it" was outfielder César Cedeño. Starting out with a paltry $3,000 bonus, he excelled in the 1970s and 1980s and frequently won Gold Glove honors for his fielding (lifetime batting average .285). In 1974, he became the first player to combine at least 20 home runs and 50 stolen bases in a single season three times in a career. Dominican fans cheered mightily when César Cedeño led the Houston Astros to their first divisional title in 1980, hitting .309 with 73 RBIs despite a battered knee. They cheered even louder in 1985. That year César went on a hitting binge for the St. Louis Cardinals: .434 in the season's final 28 games. As a result, the Cards made it into the World Series. César Cedeño was traded to the Dodgers in 1986 and cut from the roster after 37 games, one home run short of a 200-homer career.

Some of the younger Dominican players, like outfielder and infielder Pedro Guerrero, suffered severe bouts of homesickness when they first came to the United States. Guerrero, yet another son of San Pedro de Macorís, was sixteen in 1973 when he signed a Cleveland contract for a bonus of only $2,500. He had trouble adjusting to the land of ice, snow, and racial prejudice. Team owners liked to prohibit Latino players from going home to play winter ball during the off-season. The owners feared the players would get injured or be too tired to play well the following summer. Yet Latino players almost always did more poorly the next season if they did not play winter ball.

Traded to the Dodgers, Guerrero blistered the baseball in the 1980s (lifetime batting average of .305, three seasons with more than 100 RBIs). He hit two homers and shared the MVP honor in the 1981 World Series, won by Los Angeles against the Yankees four games to two. In June 1985, Pedro Guerrero set the National League record for most home runs in a month: 15. Suffering back problems and a wrist injury, he still hit .320, knocked in 87 runs, and clobbered 33 homers that year, helping the Dodgers win the division title. After an injury-plagued 1986, Pedro won the 1987 Comeback Player of the Year Award with a .338 batting average, 27 home runs, and 89 RBIs.

Homesick or not, some of today's better-paid Latin American players, fearing injury and wanting to extend their high-paid U.S. careers, decide on their own not to play winter ball. But most of them still visit their homelands as often as they can. Tony Peña, the four-time Gold Glove–winning Dominican catcher, told baseball writer Rob Ruck:

> *I go home as often as I can. I love the land, and the people there are my real friends. I care more about what people there think of me than anywhere else. I don't want them to see me any different than I was. I would not be Tony Peña if I didn't come back.* [5]

After five successive .300 seasons for the Pirates in the 1980s, Peña went on to sign a three-year $6.4 million contract with the Boston Red Sox in 1989. According to Ruck, by then Puerto Rico's Benito Santiago, 1987 National League Rookie of the Year, had overtaken Peña "as the best Latin catcher in baseball." [6] Yet Peña was still thrilling the faithful, clouting a game-winning homer for Cleveland against Boston, his former team, in the 1995 league play-off series to help the Indians into the World Series.

Today, there are more than 400 Dominicans playing in U.S. baseball, including 50 major leaguers. A similar number of Puerto Ricans are major leaguers, with Venezuelans and Mexicans a distant third and fourth among

*Dominican catcher Tony Peña exults after hitting a
game-winning homer in the 1995 AL playoffs.*

Latinos.[7] Another 400 potential stars are enrolled in Dominican baseball academies launched by major-league teams on the island. U.S. scouts now use the academies, instead of the island's baseball leagues, for recruiting prospects. Unemployed youths line up at the academies' gates every day, dreaming of fame and fortune.

Most Latino players still work for far less than white ones do, at least when starting out. A white college prospect can expect at least $150,000 for signing, compared with $4,000 for a Dominican with similar skills.[8] A Latino in his rookie minor-league year earns only $700 a month. On the other hand, Roberto Alomar, Bobby Bonilla, José Canseco, Ruben Sierra, and Danny Tartabull are among baseball's twenty highest-paid players.[9]

Mexican Fernando Valenzuela and New York City–born Puerto Rican Bobby Bonilla have lived two quite different kinds of "rags to riches" stories. Fernando Valenzuela was born in 1960 in the tiny village of Etchohuaquila on the West Coast of Mexico. His one-bedroom adobe house, with its roof of mud and sticks, had no electricity. His Mayan Indian parents farmed a half acre they owned, while their twelve children worked in the large fields of the region's wealthy farmers.

When electricity came to Etchohuaquila in 1970, Fernando began listening to radio broadcasts of Mexican Pacific Coast League games. His hero was the phenomenal home-run hitter Héctor Espino, then setting batting records that still stand today (see chapter 5). In 1976, Fernando traveled 20 miles north to pitch for his hometown team and was noticed by an organizer of Sonora state's All-Star team. At age fifteen, Fernando won the All-Star tournament's MVP award. Offered a Mexican minor-league contract of $250 for three months, he gladly accepted. It was a hard life: long dusty bus rides, players sometimes sleeping on the bus floor. But for a handful of young hopefuls, it was worth it. Valenzuela was one of the lucky ones. One day Los Angeles Dodgers scout Mike Brito was watching a game and recognized Fernando's potential. He informed Dodgers general manager Al Campanis, who obtained the eighteen-year-old pitcher's services by paying the Puebla team $120,000. Dodgers owner Walter O'Malley had long wanted to bring a Mexican star to Los Angeles in order to appeal to southern California's large Latino community.

Shipped by the Dodgers to a minor-league team in Lodi, California, Fernando missed his family and friends, especially his girlfriend, Linda Margarita Burgos. Over the winter he learned how to throw the difficult screwball, soon to become famous as "Fernando's Fadeaway." When Fernando started playing for the San Antonio team in Texas, thousands of Mexican-American fans packed the stands. They called their idol "El Jefe" ("the Chief").

At the end of the 1980 season, the Dodgers called Fernando up to help them in a tight pennant race against the Houston Astros. He appeared in ten games as a relief pitcher, allowed no runs, and struck out sixteen. Fernando won the next season's home opener with a 5-hit, 2–0 shutout against the Astros. After the last out, Los Angeles' Latino fans rose to their feet, chanting "Fernando, Fernando!" Fernandomania was born.

Valenzuela took the majors by storm, winning his first seven starts, five of them shutouts. Wherever he played, the familiar chant of "Fernando" came from the stands. Special bilingual press conferences were often held when he was scheduled to pitch, and attendance soared when Valenzuela was on the mound.

The 1981 season was a short one though, interrupted by a players' strike. During the strike, Fernando went home to Mexico to offer a baseball clinic for 25,000 children. Then he went to Washington, D.C., to have lunch with U.S. president Ronald Reagan and Mexican president José López Portillo.

After the strike ended, Fernando started the All-Star Game, allowing no runs in one inning. He went on to finish the abbreviated 1981 season with a 13–7 record, 2.48 ERA, and 180 strikeouts in 192 innings. He became the first rookie in league history to hurl eight shutouts. In postseason playoffs (because of the strike-shortened season, the top two finishers in each division competed in two rounds of playoffs) and the World Series, won by the Dodgers 4 games to 2 against the Yankees—Fernando went 3–1 in five starts. Facing three top teams, he compiled a remarkable 2.21 ERA. Not surprisingly, he won the Cy Young Award for best National League pitcher, was named Rookie of the Year, and even received a Silver Slugger Award for his hitting talents. A celebrated superstar, Fernando returned to his native Mexico a hero. There, he married his girlfriend, Linda, now a schoolteacher. Mexican radio broadcast the wedding ceremony nationwide.

For the following season, Fernando's agent asked the Dodgers for a million-dollar salary. Fernando had earned only $29,000 in his rookie year, although he picked up $300,000 in endorsements. Dodgers manager Tommy Lasorda quipped, "He wants Texas back."[10] At age twenty-one, Fernando settled for a $300,000 salary for 1982. After going 19–13 with 199 strikeouts in 286 innings and an ERA of 2.87, he again demanded a substantial raise. Arbitrators finally offered him a salary of $1 million, the highest such award ever.

During the next few years Fernando Valenzuela gained additional respect for all the community work he did in East Los Angeles barrios. A school dropout himself, he encouraged youngsters to complete their studies.

In the 1984 All-Star Game, Fernando became the seventh pitcher in history to strike out the side, fanning the American League's three best hitters—Dave Winfield, Reggie Jackson, and George Brett—in order. By 1986 he was the highest-paid Latino ever, enjoying a three-year $5.5 million salary. In that year's All-Star Game he tied a record set by Carl Hubbell, striking out five batters in a row. He still had not allowed a run in five All-Star appearances. On

Fernando Valenzuela winds up during a 1986 game against the Atlanta Braves. The Mexican pitcher drew crowds of Latino fans to Dodgers games.

September 22 he became the first Mexican to win 20 major-league games in one season, followed a couple of days later by the second, Milwaukee's Ted Higuera.

But the Dodgers' hitting failed to back up Fernando in the mid-1980s, and some of the snap seemed to go out of his fastball. Fernando's right shoulder ached wickedly. Even so, he led the National League in wins in 1986 and copped a Gold Glove award for his fielding. Moreover, he led the league in complete games that year and the next. In 1988, however, Fernando's shoulder ailment had worsened and he was placed on the disabled list, ending his string of 255 straight starts without a missed turn.

Valenzuela ended the 1990 season only 13–13, but he was still hailed in most opinion polls as baseball's greatest left-hander of the 1980s. In July 1990 he became the third Latino to hurl a no-hitter, besting St. Louis. The preceding two were Juan Marichal (1963) and Puerto Rican Juan Nieves (1987). In 1995, at age thirty, Fernando Valenzuela was still throwing hard for the San Diego Padres.

More than any other Latino player, Fernando Valenzuela awoke U.S. baseball and the mass media to the incredible potential of Latino fandom. *Time* magazine called the 1980s "the decade of the Hispanic." Actually, economic conditions for Latinos declined more than for any other group that decade, but at least Latinos were no longer invisible. And in baseball a select few finally began obtaining salaries more commensurate with their skills.

One was Bobby Bonilla, who was born in New York's South Bronx in 1963. As a boy, Bobby looked out his apartment door and saw junkies shooting up. Statistics from his neighborhood's 40th Precinct indicated roughly one robbery a day, one murder a week. But young Roberto Martín Antonio Bonilla, who dreamed every day of escaping his hazardous surroundings, had more people willing to help him out than most other poor New York City kids.

Bobby's divorced parents watched closely over him and his two younger twin sisters and younger brother. His father, Roberto Bonilla, a hardworking electrician, was born and raised in New York City, the son of Cuban–Puerto Rican parents. His mother, Regina Bonilla-Rodríguez, came to New York from Puerto Rico. To help support her family, she landed a job in the early 1970s at the run-down, hundred-year-old Lincoln Hospital—traditionally known as "the butcher shop" because of the poor health services that it provided—in the South Bronx's barrio.

It was a turbulent time when Puerto Ricans and other Latinos were protesting the inadequate care offered patients by Lincoln's medical personnel, most of whom knew no Spanish. In 1970 the Young Lords, a Puerto Rican youth movement, linked up with Lincoln Hospital patients and health workers to take over the hospital and demand full equality for minorities, including women.[11]

The social movements of the late 1960s and early 1970s won opportunities for some African Americans and Latinos. Bobby Bonilla's mother was able to attend college, earning a degree in social work at Columbia University. Eventually she became a staff psychologist at Lincoln Hospital. Young Bobby also benefited from concessions won by the social movements of the 1960s and 1970s, attending schools with special federal programs for minorities and eventually enrolling in one of the city's best integrated high schools, Lehman High.

On the streets of New York City, Bobby had grown up playing all sports, but his favorites were stickball and sponge-ball. When Bobby was nine, his parents enrolled him in a Little League. One day his father drove him by the New York Mets' Shea Stadium. Bobby said: "I'd like to play there someday."[12]

As a "model" high school, Lehman had a better-than-average faculty, many of them Jewish, like baseball coach Joe Levine. Joe got Bobby onto the varsity baseball team when he was still a ninth grader. He played Bobby in several positions and made him a switch-hitter. In Bobby's senior year, Lehman's 2,500 students raised the sum of $1,500 to pay for Bobby's trip with the U.S. amateur team, which was being sent by the U.S. Baseball Federation on a good-will trip to Scandinavia. An instructor on the trip was Pittsburgh Pirates scout Syd Thrift. Once back in the United States, Bobby signed on with the Pirates for a $10,000 bonus. He then married his high school sweetheart, Millie Quiñones, and set out to win a place in the majors. It took him awhile, but once he shortened his swing he hit his stride.

On July 3, 1987, Bonilla belted a homer batting right-handed in the third inning and then hit another homer batting left-handed four innings later, becoming the first in Pirates history ever to hit a home run from each side of the plate in the same game. In major-league history it had been done 62 times (10 of them by Hall-of-Famer Mickey Mantle). Nine days later he smashed a "mega-homer" into the upper right-field deck of Three Rivers Stadium, the first player to do that since the days of Hall-of-Famer Willie Stargell. Stargell became a good friend and adviser to the burgeoning star.

From 1987 through 1991, Bonilla batted in 483 runs, ranking ninth in the majors for that five-year period. In three of the seasons he passed the benchmark 100-RBI total. He fielded well too, intimidating runners with his strong throwing arm from the outfield. At third base he introduced the "Bonilla shuffle," jogging in place between pitches in order to improve his ability to move to either side. In 1988 he made the National League All-Star team at third base, ending an eight-year streak of future Hall-of-Famer Mike Schmidt, who acknowledged: "Right now Bonilla is the best all-around third baseman in the league."[13]

In 1990 Bonilla and his friend from minor-league days, Barry Bonds, blistered the baseball and led the Pirates to their first division title in eleven years. Bonds and Bonilla finished one-two in the MVP voting. For the first time in Pirates history, more than 2 million fans attended home games. But Bonilla was having contract problems with the owners of the Pirates' management. In the winter he was offered a $1.25 million contract, but other players in the majors made more while producing less. In 1991 he decided to play out his option and become a free agent (a player who chooses the option of keeping his old contract for a second year can become a free agent). Fortunately for him, Bobby had another good season in 1991, producing a .302 batting average with 18 home runs, 100 RBIs, and a league-leading 44 doubles, helping the Pirates to run away with the pennant by 14 games and making him an attractive "buy" on the free market.

Five teams entered one of baseball's most frenetic bidding wars in history to gain Bonilla's services. The New York Mets won with a $29 million five-year contract offer and a $1.5 million bonus for signing. This made Bonilla the highest-paid player in any sport ever, although he fell to second place behind Ryne Sandberg of the Cubs two weeks later. It was a year when Latino superstars finally gained the economic rewards they deserved. José Canseco, for example, signed with the Oakland A's for $23.8 million over five years.

Bobby's childhood dream of playing at Shea had finally become a reality. When asked if the big-bucks pressure might be too much for him on the Mets' home field, Bonilla said: "There is no pressure in baseball. Pressure is growing up in the South Bronx."[14] When starting out with the Mets, Bonilla promised his former public schools $500 each for every run he batted in—to go toward incentive programs and sports equipment for the students. At first he excluded Lehman, since it had fired his old coach, Joe Levine. But then he changed his mind, noting "it wasn't the kids' fault."[15]

Despite this auspicious start, Bobby fell on hard times with Mets fans. His first two seasons he hit only .249 and .265, although belting 34 homers in 1993. He suffered a debilitating shoulder injury and grew cranky with the New York press and teammates. In the strike-abbreviated 1994 season, though, he bounced back, setting a club record of at least 1 RBI in 9 straight games and hitting .290 with 20 homers. When the strike ended in 1995, Bobby Bonilla went on a hitting rampage. He hit .325 with 18 homers and 53 RBIs for the Mets before being traded to Baltimore in late July. Truly, there seemed to be life after the South Bronx.

9
nueve

BASEBALL'S

LATINO

ACCENT

TODAY

Given the prominence of Hispanic-American and Latin American players, it seems that baseball will increasingly take on a Spanish accent.

— Baseball writers John S. Bowman and Joel Zoss[1]

Today, Latino and African-American players account for more than a third of all major leaguers. Moreover, they often lead the leagues in several categories of play. A glance at any major- or minor-league team roster turns up countless Latino surnames.

Whether all fans realize it or not, familiar names in the strike-abbreviated 1994–95 seasons were just some of the many talented Latinos born here or in Latin America enriching "our national pastime." Among them were league leaders in both major leagues: batting title winners like Julio Franco (1991, American League), Edgar Martínez (1992, 1995, American League), and Andrés Galarraga (1993, National League); and home-run sluggers and RBI leaders like José Canseco (American League home-run titles in 1988 and 1991, RBI title in 1988), Juan González (two consecutive American League home-run titles in 1992–93), and Rubén Sierra (RBI title in 1989).

Latinos excelled in pitching as well, with top ERA hurlers like Steve Ontiveros, who won the American League ERA title in 1994, and Dennis Martínez (see chapter 7). Latino strikeout kings included the Dominican Republic's José Rijo, 1993 National League strikeout leader and 1990 World Series MVP. Venezuelan Wilson Alvarez started his brilliant career with the Chicago White Sox in 1991 by throwing a no-hitter. Fireballing Florida-born José Mesa of the Cleveland Indians set a major-league record in August 1995 with his 37th save in 37 attempts in a single season.

On June 3, 1995, in San Diego, Dominican Pedro J. Martínez of the Montreal Expos became only the second player in history to start a game and throw perfect no-hit

Puerto Rican Edgar Martínez waits for a pitch. In 1995, he won his second batting title; he hit .357 with 29 home runs and 81 extra-base hits.

baseball past the ninth inning. The twenty-three-year-old right-hander allowed a leadoff double in the tenth and was replaced by Dominican forkball artist Mel Rojas. Rojas, the strong relief hurler with 10-plus saves in each of the preceding three seasons finished the one-hitter, won by the Expos 1-0. Six weeks later Pedro's brother Ramón Martínez tossed a no-hitter for the Dodgers against the Florida Marlins.

Meanwhile, Latinos hit and ran bases as well as ever. In June 1995, Colorado's Andrés Galarraga, born in Caracas, Venezuela, became the fourth major leaguer to homer in three consecutive innings in an 11-3 wipeout of the San Diego Padres at Jack Murphy Stadium. In the 1995 post-season playoffs, batting champion Edgar Martínez, born in New York and raised in Puerto Rico, thrilled the nation's television viewers with his extra-bases hits in the clutch, including an extra-inning grand slam shot to dead center field that buried the Yankees. The Marlins' rookie sensation Quilvio Veras led the majors in stolen bases with 56.

The list of Latino stars is too long to give here, but a spring 1995 snapshot of rosters included these familiar names (1994 batting average or won-loss record in parentheses; you can find more-recent statistics in standard baseball guides that appear every spring):

Rick Aguilera (1–4, with 23 saves)
José Félix (.303)
Félix Fermín (.317)
Roberto Alomar (.306)
Alex Fernández (11–7)
Sandy Alomar, Jr. (.288)
Tony Fernández (.279)
Moisés Alou (.339)
Andrés Galarraga (.319)
René Arocha (4–4)
Juan González (.275)
Bobby Ayala (4–3)
Luis González (.273)
Carlos Baerga (.314)
Ozzie Guillén (.288)
Gerónimo Berroa (.306)
José Guzmán (2–2)
Bobby Bonilla (.290)
Juan Guzmán (12–11)
Andújar Cedeño (.263)
Roberto Hernández (4–4)
Will Cordero (.294)
Roberto Kelly (.293)

Javier López (.245)
Luis López (.277)
Pedro A. Martínez (3–2)
Pedro J. Martínez (11–5)
Ramón Martínez (12–7)
Tino Martínez (.261)
Raúl Mondesi (.306)
Bobby Muñoz (7–5)
Pedro Muñoz (.295)
Rafael Palmeíro (.319)
Melido Pérez (9–4)

Luis Polonia (.311)
Manny Ramírez (.269)
Henry Rodríguez (.268)
Ivan Rodríguez (.298)
Rey Sánchez (.285)
Benito Santiago (.273)
Luis Sojo (.277)
Sammy Sosa (.300)
José Viscaino (.256)
Omar Vizquel (.273)

As baseball has been "Latinizing," U.S. organized baseball, the U.S. Labor Department, and the INS (Immigration and Naturalization Service) have developed a quota system limiting each team to under twenty-four work visas a year for foreign-born players to "hold positions that they argue cannot be filled by U.S. citizens" in either the major or minor leagues.[2] Baseball writers Michael Oleksak and Mary Oleksak have observed: "Like migrant farm workers they receive temporary visas to go north to supplement the local work force."[3] Usually, there are not enough visas to satisfy the demand. In 1994, 13 of the top 48 vote getters for the All Star Game were Latinos, a whopping 27 percent! If the immigration doors were ever to open wider to Latino ballplayers, they could conceivably become a *majority* of All-Stars.

That may seem unlikely in light of the immigrant bashing sweeping the nation. In 1995 there were new proposed laws in Congress that would radically reduce the number of legal immigrants and take away rights granted them under earlier laws. But baseball owners often act like the owners of the nation's agribusinesses. They seek and usually get special treatment for "their" immigrants![4]

Despite the impressive presence of Latino players, superstars included, racism has by no means died. In 1987 and 1992 two scandals involving racist remarks by leading baseball executives led baseball aficionados to despair about the possibility of ever truly integrating baseball. The first happened in the year of the hundredth anniversary of baseball's first official color line and on the day of the fortieth anniversary of Jackie Robinson's rookie year. Los Angeles Dodgers vice president and general manager Al Campanis granted an interview to Ted Koppel for the ABC television show "Nightline." Koppel asked Campanis if prejudice was the reason there were so few black managers, coaches, and executives. "No, I don't believe it's prejudice," Campanis replied. "I truly believe that they may not have some of the necessities to be, let's say, a field manager, or perhaps a general manager."

Flabbergasted, Koppel suggested this sounded like the "garbage we were hearing forty years ago about players." Campanis responded with a rambling set of remarks that only made matters worse:

> No, it's not garbage, Mr. Koppel, because I played on a college team, and the center fielder was black.... why are black men, or black people, not good swimmers? Because they don't have the buoyancy.... I have never said that blacks are not intelligent.... They are gifted with great musculature ... they're fleet of foot, and this is why there are a lot of black major-league baseball players. Now, as far as having the background to become club presidents, or presidents of a bank, I don't know.[5]

A national uproar occurred. Two days later Campanis was fired.

Then, in the fall of 1992, Marge Schott, chief owner of the Cincinnati Reds, reportedly called one of her star outfielders a "million-dollar nigger" and used the phrase "sneaky Jew bastards."[6] The press had a field day, revealing other alleged racist behavior by Schott. Some, including Schott, suspected sexism in singling out a woman for racial insults that male baseball executives and players had been hurling for decades. Schott claimed that her alleged racism was one big media lie.

In the momentary absence of a sitting baseball commissioner,[7] a ten-member Executive Council of Major League Baseball launched an investigation. The Council, consisting mainly of team owners and executives, delayed awhile before finally censuring Schott "in the strongest terms for her use of racially and ethnically insensitive language." It directed her "to attend and complete multicultural training programs" and fined her the maximum possible: $25,000. Finally, it suspended Schott for one year, beginning March 1, 1993.[8]

Before the Schott scandal became public, perhaps even to head it off, Cincinnati general manager Jim Bowden named a Latino, Tony Pérez, new team manager. The highly respected Cuban-born slugger was incredibly popular in Cincinnati, where he had helped spark the 1970s World Champion Big Red Machine. But after only 44 games (20 wins) of the 1993 season, Bowden fired Pérez. Players and fans cried "foul!" To protest Pérez's removal, Coach Ron Oester handed in his resignation.

Pérez, who during the course of Schott's earlier difficulties had spoken kindly about her, remained silent. Later, however, he indicated he had been "set up" as manager to help improve Schott's image, and that Schott, who met with Bowden two days before his firing, had surely had a say in his removal.[9] One baseball commentator echoed a widespread sentiment: "Ironically, the real victim of Marge's suspension so far seems to be the Latino, Pérez."[10]

After the Campanis and Schott scandals, the number of nonwhites holding down jobs in baseball front offices shot up nearly tenfold to more than 15 percent. The first African-American league president was named in 1989: former first baseman Bill White.[11] But African Americans and Latinos continued to be very underrepresented in the choicest positions of major-league baseball. In 1995, team owners were still all-white, and there was only one non-

white general manager, Houston's Bob Watson, who was appointed New York Yankees general manager after the season's end. The only nonwhite managers on the field were Montreal's Felipe Alou (1994 National League Manager of the Year), and San Francisco's Dusty Baker, Toronto's Cito Gaston, and Colorado's Don Baylor (1995 National League Manager of the Year).[12]

Both Latinos and African Americans are also underrepresented in the Hall of Fame. As early as 1969, the American Civil Liberties Union asked baseball commissioner Bowie Kuhn to open up the Hall equally to players of all races, but Kuhn's legal counsel asserted that "Cooperstown is a private club" not covered by civil rights laws.[13] In 1971 Satchel Paige was the first African-American admitted to the Hall. From 1971 to 1977 a special Committee on Negro Baseball Leagues elected nine Negro-league players to the Hall of Fame, including Cuban great Martín Dihigo. But there remain only half a dozen Latinos in the Hall—and that's including Reggie Jackson.[14]

In the middle of the 1994 season, new troubles erupted with the longest strike in sports history. Players, instead of getting a fair chunk of baseball's expanding economic pie—revenues from TV, advertising, and the computerized media superhighway—saw their old contract agreements being tossed into the garbage bin. So the Players Association announced a strike.[15]

Once again, baseball reflected the larger society. The actions of club owners against the players reinforced a general push against workers' rights that had reduced wages

Montreal Expos manager Felipe Alou watches the action of the 1995 All-Star Game. He was the 1994 National League Manager of the Year. Despite the success of Latino players and managers, there are no Latinos in top front-office positions in the major leagues.

and slashed the nation's total membership in labor unions from more than 30 percent of the workforce in the 1960s to less than 15 percent by 1994. In response to the baseball strike, team owners suspended their contributions to the players' pension fund, cancelled the 1994 World Series, jettisoned the four-year 1990 agreement with the union, and brought in amateurish "replacement players" for the 1995 season's spring training. New York's *Village Voice* sportswriter Allen St. John wrote about the owners' use of replacement players: "The real message behind Scabfest '95, one that is being heard loud and clear by management all over the country, is that if you can replace Frank Thomas and Barry Bonds, you can replace anyone."[16]

Not one player from any of the teams' regular rosters broke ranks to join the replacement players. This player unity paid off. The National Labor Relations Board (NLRB) obtained an injunction to force the owners back to the terms of the 1990 agreement and end the strike. The federal judge who granted the injunction was a forty-year-old Latina, Puerto Rican Sonia Sotomayor. The first Latino ever to be appointed to the federal bench in heavily Puerto Rican and Dominican New York City, Judge Sotomayor ruled that the owners had engaged in unfair bargaining by suspending the old agreements' salary arbitration, free-agent bidding, and anticollusion clauses.

It was a great victory not just for the Players Association but for organized labor as a whole. As Kevin Baker pointed out in an opinion column for the *New York Times*:

> *Most of the players who are millionaires are also white, male, politically conservative—and very talented. If even their most fundamental rights can be trampled by a cartel of 28 club owners while the Government looks on, how will the rest of us fare in the brave new economy?[17]*

No new agreements were reached in baseball, however, and people feared new player strikes or owner lockouts ahead. Fans also responded negatively to the strike, often wondering why "millionaire players" were not satisfied.

During the 1994–95 strike, many commentators wondered aloud about baseball's survival. Some speculated about the future relationship between strong Latin American and Japanese leagues and U.S. baseball. There was talk of a new major-league franchise being created in Mexico City. At least twenty-five U.S. major-league players had jumped to play ball in Japan in recent years, and the economic rivalry between the two financial superpowers was heating up. But as former Detroit Tigers and Cincinnati Reds manager Sparky Anderson once said, "We've tried and tried to ruin this game and we just can't do it."[18]

Because of their disgust with the prolonged strike, many fans did not show up for major-league games in the 1995 season and went to local minor-league games instead. Major-league owners tried various gimmicks to bring the fans back, including reduced ticket prices and special gifts. They also sought to appeal to specialized "niche markets" among the fans. Often, this meant appealing directly to the growing Latino population. The New York Yankees sponsored an "Hispanic Awards Night" for 100 top Latino high school students. At least half a dozen major-league teams were already offering Spanish-language radio broadcasts of their games.

Latino players were performing better than ever, with a new crop of stars emerging early in the 1995 season, including Minnesota's 1995 Rookie of the Year, Marty Córdoba, Cubs rookie pitcher Jaime Navarro, Mets rookie third baseman Edgardo Alfonzo, Expos rookie pitcher Carlos Pérez (brother of Yankees hurler Melido Pérez), and Florida Marlins' rookie second baseman Quilvio Veras.

Moreover, the old pattern of Latino-dominant teams moving up in the standings reasserted itself in the 1995 season. Almost all the winners of the major-leagues' six divisions had starting lineups with three or more Latino players. The multicultural Cleveland club, the American League

Central Division champion, played sizzling .694 baseball before losing the World Series. In Cleveland's infield were Venezuelan shortstop Omar Vizquel, Puerto Rican second baseman Carlos Baerga, and catchers Tony Peña and Sandy Alomar, Jr. In an outstanding .300-hitting outfield was the twenty-three-year-old 1994 rookie sensation from the Dominican Republic, Manny Ramírez (107 RBIs). Cleveland's pitching staff featured ace reliever José Mesa and "El Presidente," the ageless starter Dennis Martínez (see chapter 7). Both were near the top of the league in ERA. A third of the Toronto Blue Jays' 200-player organization today comes from the Dominican Republic or other Caribbean Basin countries. Frequent pennant winners like Toronto, Los Angeles, and Oakland have featured a disproportionate number of Latinos on their rosters for years.[19]

Baseball schools in Latin America have superseded the old farm system for developing future baseball stars. Seventeen of twenty-six major-league teams run special training facilities in the Dominican Republic alone.[20]

But baseball cannot be played without baseballs. The ultimate dependence of U.S. baseball on Latinos shows up when you follow the white ball back to its origins. Women in Central America and Haiti stitch major-league baseballs. They earn about a dollar a day for more than ten hours of work on their feet. They are not allowed even to talk about forming a union, and outside inspectors are not permitted to enter the places where they work.

Ever since the 1950s, white Americans have been moving to the suburbs, and major-league baseball has not been far behind them. Using taxpayers' monies, team owners

Dennis Martínez prepares to deliver a pitch against the Atlanta Braves in game six of the 1995 World Series. The Nicaraguan ace threw a perfect game in 1991, and he is one of only six pitchers to have won 100 or more games in both major leagues.

have created impressive new stadiums near densely populated suburban areas. Washington Senators president Calvin Griffith (son of Clark Griffith) confided to American League owners the reason for his moving the team to Minneapolis in 1961: "The trend in Washington is getting to be all colored," he said.[21] At a Minneapolis Lions Club luncheon he added:

> *I'll tell you why we came to Minnesota. It was when I*
> *found out you only had fifteen thousand blacks*
> *here....We came here because you've got good,*
> *hardworking white people here.*[22]

In 1961–62, each league expanded to ten teams. By 1993, each had fourteen teams in three divisions.

Inner-city fans have found it increasingly difficult to afford the prices of baseball tickets. Big-city stadiums have often stood half empty. Recently, the number of black professional athletes has risen in football and basketball and dropped in baseball. African-American fan interest in baseball is on the decline, although Latino fan interest is still strong.

The Supreme Court's reversal of affirmative action in 1995, combined with growing poverty among nonwhites, does not augur much hope for interracial harmony in the United States. Latinos and African Americans, even though competing for scarce jobs, are still leading the way together in the effort to abolish racism in U.S. baseball. They will not succeed unless society as a whole changes. If major-league baseball is to last "forever," then racism in the United States will have to be uprooted forever, too.

SOURCE NOTES

PREFACE

1. The 1980 Census officially introduced the term *Hispanic* to replace *Latino* in part to depoliticize the Latinos' empowerment movements of the 1960s and 1970s. In real life, of course, individual Latinos identify themselves as American or as, for example, Puerto Rican, Dominican, Nicaraguan—or both. For more on this, see James D. Cockcroft, *The Hispanic Struggle for Social Justice* (New York: Franklin Watts, 1994), 9–12, 85–100; Hedda Garza, *Latinas: Hispanic Women in the United States* (New York: Franklin Watts, 1995), 11–13.

CHAPTER 1

1. Quoted in Donn Rogosin, *Invisible Men: Life in Baseball's Negro Leagues* (New York: Atheneum, 1983), 159. Besides Rogosin, this chapter is based on John S. Bowman and Joel Zoss, *Diamonds in the Rough: The Untold History of Baseball* (New York: Macmillan, 1989); Tom Gilbert, *Baseball and the Color Line* (New York: Franklin Watts, 1995); Nicolás Kanellos, ed., *The Hispanic-American Almanac* (Detroit: Gale Research, 1993); Jacob Margolies, *The Negro Leagues: The Story of Black Baseball* (New York: Franklin Watts, 1993); Michael Oleksak and Mary Adams Oleksak, *Béisbol: Latin Americans and the Grand Old Game* (Grand Rapids, MI: Masters Press, 1991); Robert Peterson, *Only the Ball Was White* (New York: McGraw Hill, 1970); Paula J. Pettavino and Geralyn Pye, *Sport in Cuba: The Diamond in the Rough* (Pittsburgh: University of Pittsburgh Press, 1994); Rob Ruck, *The Tropic of Baseball: Baseball in the Dominican Republic* (Westport, CT: Meckler, 1991); and Jules Tygiel, *Baseball's Great Experiment: Jackie Robinson and His Legacy* (New York: Oxford University Press, 1983).

2. Quoted in Ruck, 35.

3. Quoted in Gilbert, 68; see also, Art Rust, Jr., *"Get That Nigger Off the Field"* (New York: Delacorte Press, 1976), 13–14.

4. Quoted in Peterson, 62; Gilbert, 107.

5. McGraw later attempted signing up African-American players by claiming they were Cuban immigrants. In 1917 an African-American outfielder named John Donaldson turned down a $10,000 offer "to go to Cuba, change his name, and report to a club in the New York State League"—quoted in Howard Senzel, *Baseball and the Cold War: Being a Soliloquy on the Necessity of Baseball* (New York: Harcourt Brace Jovanovich, 1977), 257.

6. Noted in Bowman and Zoss, 127.

7. Quoted in Gilbert, 42; 67.

8. Although there are hardly any *documented* cases of African Americans "passing" as whites in the major leagues, a sportswriter in the early 1940s acknowledged that "It is no secret that players of suspected Negro parentage have appeared in big league games." Quoted in Gilbert, 104.

9. In 1906, Foster, playing for Chicago's all-black Leland Giants, pushed for and won a new financial arrangement to help his underpaid black teammates. He persuaded club owner Frank Leland to share gate receipts fifty-fifty with the players, an unheard of arrangement for team owners who ran baseball like their personal kingdom. Foster continued the unique gate-sharing practice when he became manager of the Chicago American Giants, a team that played well in the Negro leagues for years to come.

10. Ruth's behavior was even stranger in light of *his* sometimes being called a "nigger" because of his dark complexion and rumored African-American ancestry. Ty Cobb, an ardent racist, once refused to share a Georgia hunting lodge with Ruth because "I have never slept under the same roof with a nigger, and I'm not going to start here in my own native state of Georgia." Quoted in Paul Dickson, *Baseball's Greatest Quotations* (New York: HarperPerennial, 1992), 85. For more, see Margolies, 20–23; Oleksak and Oleksak, 23, 34; Pettavino and Pye, 249; Senzel, 257.

11. Sportswriter Fred Lieb later wrote that Cobb and "1920s' stars 'Gabby' Street, Rogers Hornsby, and Tris Speaker all told him that they were members of the Ku Klux Klan"—quoted in Tygiel, 32. For more on Cobb's racism and his visit to Cuba, see Al Stump, *Cobb: A Biography* (Chapel Hill, N.C.: Algonquin Books, 1994). Babe Ruth and Honus Wagner later acknowledged that Pop Lloyd was the greatest player they had ever seen. Lloyd, along with other underpaid black and Latino players, frequently played in Cuba.

12. Quoted in Oleksak and Oleksak, 22.

13. Ibid.

14. Noted in Bruce Brown, "Cuban Baseball," *The Atlantic*, 253:6 (June 1984), 111; Oleksak and Oleksak, 26, 253.

15. Later, as a player-manager, Méndez led the Kansas City Monarchs to three straight Negro National League pennants. In 1926 he died after a sudden illness, his career cut short at age thirty-eight, some twenty years before the color line was challenged by Jackie Robinson.

16. Noted in Oleksak and Oleksak, 26.

17. Noted in Walter M. Langford, *Legends of Baseball* (South Bend, IN: Diamond Communications, 1987), 218–19; see also Leonard Koppett, *The Man in the Dugout: Baseball's Top Managers and How They Got That Way* (New York: Crown, 1993), 178–84.

18. Quoted in Rogosin, 159–60.

19. Quoted in Oleksak and Oleksak, 44.

20. Noted in *Encyclopedia Americana* (New York: Americana Corporation, 1964), 305k.

CHAPTER 2

1. John Krich, *El Béisbol: Travels through the Pan-American Pastime* (New York: Atlantic Monthly Press, 1990), 191. Principal sources for this chapter are Ken Burns and Geoffrey C. Ward, *Baseball: An Illustrated History* (New York: Knopf, 1994); Bob Carroll, *Baseball Between the Lies: The Hype, Hokum, and Humbug of America's Favorite Pastime* (New York: Perigee, 1993); James D. Cockcroft, *The Hispanic Struggle for Social Justice* (New York: Franklin Watts, 1994); Tom Gilbert, *Baseball and the Color Line* (New York: Franklin Watts, 1995);Dan Gutman, *Baseball Babylon* (New York: Penguin Books, 1992); Krich; Jacob Margolies, *The Negro Leagues: The Story of Black Baseball* (New York: Franklin Watts, 1993); Harold Peterson, *The Man Who Invented Baseball* (New York: Scribner, 1973); Paula J. Pettavino and Geralyn Pye, *Sport in Cuba: The Diamond in the Rough* (Pittsburgh: University of Pittsburgh Press, 1994); Benjamin G. Rader, *Baseball: A History of America's Game* (Urbana: University of Illinois Press, 1992); and Bob Ruck, *The Tropic of Baseball: Baseball in the Dominican Republic* (Westport, CT: Meckler, 1991).

2. Quoted in Alan M. Klein, "Culture, Politics, and Baseball in the Dominican Republic," *Latin American Perspectives*, 22:3 (Summer 1995), 113–14.

3. Gutman, 331.

4. Quoted in James D. Cockcroft, *Latin America: History, Politics, and U.S. Policy* (Chicago: Nelson-Hall, 1995), 34.

5. The British game of cricket was once suspected of being a parent of baseball. In reality, though, cricket seems to have been a nineteenth-century modification of baseball rather than the other way around.

6. By the time of the American Revolution, some form of "rounders," or "town ball," was being played throughout the colonies—and not just by girls. Religious voices often cried out against it. Indeed, a 1797 law in Fayetteville, North Carolina, prohibited African Americans from playing ball on Sundays! Nonetheless, slaves in the South, free blacks in the North, and people just about everywhere played one or another form of baseball.

7. One such club was New York City's Knickerbocker Base Ball Club, established in 1845. The name Knickerbocker, after one of the first Dutch settlers in the days of Peter Stuyvesant, represented a claim to social status.

8. Later, in 1867, the African-American Pythian Base Ball Club of Philadelphia attempted to join the all-white NABBP. NABBP officials said they refused the Pythians in order to avoid "division of feeling" and "any subject having a political bearing" (Gilbert, 22). This reference to subjects *other than skin color* was a typical evasive tactic used by "northern-style" racists who had just fought in the Civil War, after all, to end slavery and supposedly introduce equal rights. In 1869, in a baseball game advertised as the first racially "mixed" match, the Pythians beat the all-white City Items.

9. Quoted in Gilbert, 27. Many whites knew that African-American votes had made up the margin of victory for President-elect General Ulysses S. Grant and that these were the days of "Reconstruction"—the long overdue opening of a "small window of opportunity" for at least some blacks.

10. Teams hired African-American mascots for the amusement of players or "because rubbing an African American's head was considered to be good luck" (Gilbert, 76). As the color line was once again firmly drawn by 1887, some Latino and African-American ballplayers started playing for the first two African-American baseball leagues, the Southern League of Colored Baseballists and the League of Colored Baseball Clubs (1886–87). Both folded, although the second one was briefly admitted into the white minor leagues before its collapse. Then Organized Baseball recemented the color line in the minors, although some teams still hired Latinos and African Americans on an individual basis.

11. In baseball, only a few superstars—a Cap Anson, Ty Cobb, or Christy Mathewson—were allowed to make a decent salary. The owners ran the game like feudal lords overseeing lowly serfs. Occasionally,

things went poorly for the owners. In 1891–92, an economic depression caused many baseball leagues, including the American Association, to collapse. With no need for so many ballplayers, the small number of African Americans or Latinos who had slipped through the cracks to play on white minor-league teams dropped to almost zero—further consolidating the color line.

12. In 1886, the Chinese had been officially excluded from further entry, and by 1907 the Japanese had also been told to stay home. The Mexicans' ancestors had worked and lived here long before the arrival of the English, but their lands had been stolen by aggressive white settlers who had moved westward in the years leading up to the 1846–48 U.S.-Mexico War, when Mexico surrendered half its territory—today's southwestern United States, including California.

13. Quoted in Alfredo Castañeda et al., eds., *Mexican Americans and Educational Change* (New York: Arno Press, 1974), 24–25, and Francesco Cordasco and Eugene Bucchioni, eds., *The Puerto Rican Community and Its Children on the Mainland: A Source Book for Teachers, Social Workers and Other Professionals* (Metuchen, N.J.: The Scarecrow Press, 1982), 265.

14. Quoted in Pettavino and Pye, 60. Sometimes, to deliberately provoke Spanish authorities, Cubans referred to baseball as *pelota americana* (American ball).

15. Quoted in John S. Bowman and Joel Zoss, *Diamonds in the Rough: The Untold History of Baseball* (New York: Macmillan, 1989), 403.

16. Quoted in Alan M. Klein, "Culture, Politics, and Baseball in the Dominican Republic," *Latin American Perspectives*, 22:3 (Summer 1995), 124.

17. Quoted in Ruck, 27.

18. Ibid., 32.

19. Cuban worker quoted in Pettavino and Pye, 63.

20. Howard Senzel, *Baseball and the Cold War: Being a Soliloquy on the Necessity of Baseball* (New York: Harcourt Brace Jovanovich, 1977), 256.

CHAPTER 3

1. Quoted in Oleksak and Oleksak, 30. Besides the Oleksaks' book, principal sources for this chapter are Ken Burns and Geoffrey C. Ward, *Baseball: An Illustrated History* (New York: Knopf, 1994); James D. Cockcroft, *The Hispanic Struggle for Social Justice* (New York: Franklin Watts, 1994); Hedda Garza, *African Americans and Jewish Americans* (New York: Franklin Watts, 1995) and *Without Regard to*

Race (New York: Franklin Watts, 1995); Tom Gilbert, *Baseball and the Color Line* (New York: Franklin Watts, 1995); Dan Gutman, *Baseball Babylon* (New York: Penguin Books, 1992); John Krich, *El Béisbol: Travels through the Pan-American Pastime* (New York: Atlantic Monthly Press, 1990); Jacob Margolies, *The Negro Leagues: The Story of Black Baseball* (New York: Franklin Watts, 1993); Robert Peterson, *Only the Ball Was White* (New York: McGraw-Hill, 1970); Paula J. Pettavino and Geralyn Pye, *Sport in Cuba: The Diamond in the Rough* (Pittsburgh: University of Pittsburgh Press, 1994); Benjamin G. Rader, *Baseball: A History of America's Game* (Urbana: University of Illinois Press, 1992); Donn Rogosin, *Invisible Men: Life in Baseball's Negro Leagues* (New York: Atheneum, 1983); Bob Ruck, *The Tropic of Baseball: Baseball in the Dominican Republic* (Westport, CT: Meckler, 1991).

2. For more on this, see Hedda Garza, *Women in Medicine* (New York: Franklin Watts, 1994) and *Barred From the Bar* (Danbury, CT: Franklin Watts, 1996).

3. For more on this, see Rodolfo Acuña, *Occupied America: A History of Chicanos* (New York: Harper & Row, 3d ed., 1988) and Cockcroft.

4. Quoted in Garza, *African Americans and Jewish Americans*, 55.

5. The owners of the Yankees and Cardinals took advantage of baseball's cartel status to build up their profitable dynasties. The Yankees were the American League champions almost every year between 1921 and 1964 (29 pennants). The National League Cardinals finished first nine times and second six times from 1926 to 1946. Yankees general manager Edward G. Barrow purchased several minor-league and big-league stars. Cardinals general manager Branch Rickey created the first extensive farm system. Barrow added a farm system of his own in the 1930s.

6. Quoted in Margolies, 29.

7. Quoted in John S. Bowman and Joel Zoss, 128. For more on Jews in baseball, see Garza, *African Americans and Jewish Americans*, and Hank Greenberg, *The Story of My Life* (New York: Times Books, 1989).

8. Quoted in Greenberg, 5.

9. Ibid., xiv.

10. Noted in Cockcroft, 73.

11. Players' salaries were cut, night baseball was introduced, and from 1934 until 1939, the ball-club owners banned radio broadcasts of games, hoping more people would come to the stadiums. To stimulate public interest, All Star Games and Most Valuable Player awards were introduced and, in 1936, the Baseball Hall of Fame was inaugurated in Cooperstown.

12. Noted by Margolies, 60.

13. Quoted in Rogosin, 168.

14. Quoted in Rogosin, 181.

15. Tygiel, *Baseball's Great Experiment: Jackie Robinson and His Legacy* (New York: Oxford University Press, 1983),182.

16. For more, see Greenberg, xii.

17. Quoted in Tygiel, 32–33.

18. Ibid., 33.

19. Ibid., 34.

20. For more details, see Cockcroft; Donald R. McCoy and Richard T. Ruetten, *Quest and Response* (Wichita: University Press of Kansas, 1978), 4–6; Howard Zinn, *A People's History of the United States* (New York: HarperPerennial, 1980), 398-426.

21. Quoted in Garza, *African Americans and Jewish Americans*, 107.

CHAPTER 4

1. Quoted in Paul Dickson, *Baseball's Greatest Quotations* (New York: HarperPerennial, 1992), 366. Except where otherwise noted, this chapter is based on information from Hedda Garza, *African Americans and Jewish Americans* (New York: Franklin Watts, 1995); Tom Gilbert, *Baseball and the Color Line* (New York: Franklin Watts, 1995); Dan Gutman, *Baseball Babylon* (New York: Penguin Books, 1992); Jacob Margolies, *The Negro Leagues: The Story of Black Baseball* (New York: Franklin Watts, 1993); Orestes Miñoso, and Fernando Fernandez and Robert Kleinfelder, *Extra Innings: My Life in Baseball* (Chicago: Regnery Gateway, 1983); Michael Oleksak and Mary Adams Oleksak, *Béisbol: Latin Americans and the Grand Old Game* (Grand Rapids, MI: Masters Press, 1991); Benjamin G. Rader, *Baseball: A History of America's Game* (Urbana: University of Illinois Press, 1992); Donn Rogosin, *Invisible Men: Life in Baseball's Negro Leagues* (New York: Atheneum, 1983); Jules Tygiel, *Baseball's Great Experiment: Jackie Robinson and His Legacy* (New York: Oxford University Press, 1983).

2. Quoted in Rogosin, 182.

3. Quoted in Gutman, 335.

4. Quoted in Tygiel, 35.

5. Quoted in Rogosin, 181.

6. Quoted in Rader, 149; Gilbert, 128.

7. Quoted in Tygiel, 38-39.

8. Ibid., 39.

9. Ibid., 20.

10. Quoted in Rogosin, 193.

11. Quoted in Hank Greenberg. *The Story of My Life* (New York: Times Books, 1989), 223.

12. Quoted in Tygiel, 199.

13. For the full story of how black tank battalions, called the Panthers, led white infantry units into some of the war's turning-point battles, see Lou Potter, *Liberators* (New York: Harcourt Brace Jovanovich, 1992), 58–154, and Hedda Garza, *Without Regard to Race* (New York: Franklin Watts, 1995), 49–51.

14. Quoted in Tygiel, 45.

15. Ibid., 43.

16. Both quotes from Tygiel, 45.

17. Quoted in Tygiel, 208.

18. For more on this, see James D. Cockcroft, *Latinos in the Struggle for Equal Education* (New York: Franklin Watts, 1995).

19. Quoted in Donald R. McCoy and Richard T. Ruetten, *Quest and Response* (Wichita: University Press of Kansas, 1978), 48.

20. For more on this conversion of the Soviet Union from ally to enemy, see Howard Zinn, *A People's History of the United States* (New York: HarperPerennial, 1980), 417–19.

21. Quoted in Oleksak and Oleksak, 53.

22. Quoted in Rader, 141.

23. Quoted in Tygiel, 77.

24. Quoted in Rogosin, 203.

25. Rickey was fond of one story in particular. In 1904, when Rickey was starting out as a coach for Wesleyan College in Ohio, a young black player was denied admission to a segregated hotel. Rickey let him sleep on a cot in his room. Rickey claimed that, seeing the boy's hurt, he decided then and there to change the situation someday if he could. However, later in life, Rickey never made a move to desegregate the stands or the press box at Sportsman's Park in St. Louis. In fact, for years the stadium remained the only segregated field in the majors. Furthermore, Rickey, famous for his scouting, had never had a word to say about the exciting black-white barnstorming games that took place right under his nose in Sportsman's Park.

26. Quoted in Rogosin, 209.

27. Quoted in Margolies, 52.

28. Quoted in Gilbert, 109.

29. Quoted in Tygiel, 146. In Nashua, Newcombe and Campanella and their wives were welcomed and given free choice of places to live and eat. Wright and Partlow also were also well received by the 50,000 residents of the French Canadian city of Three Rivers, playing out the 1946 season in the Class C Canadian League.

30. Quoted in Rogosin, 216.

31. Quoted in Tygiel, 120.

32. Tygiel, 122.

33. Gilbert, 141.

34. Quoted in Tygiel, 163.

35. Ibid., 163.

36. Ibid., 170.

37. Ibid., 185.

38. Ibid., 182.

39. Ibid., 184.

40. Ibid., 188.

41. Ibid., 253.

42. Quoted in Garza, *African Americans and Jewish Americans*, 118.

43. Quotes are from Greenberg, 191.

44. Quoted in Oleksak and Oleksak, 54–55.

45. Quoted in Tygiel, 323.

46. Ibid., 169.

47. Ibid., 309.

CHAPTER 5

1. Quoted in Art Rust, Jr., *"Get That Nigger Off the Field"* (New York: Delacorte Press, 1976), 193. This chapter's main sources are Thomas W. Gilbert, *Roberto Clemente* (New York: Chelsea House, 1991); Dan Gutman, *Baseball Babylon* (New York: Penguin Books, 1992); John Krich, *El Béisbol: Travels through the Pan-American Pastime* (New York: Atlantic Monthly Press, 1990); Michael Oleksak and Mary Adams Oleksak, *Béisbol: Latin Americans and the Grand Old Game* (Grand Rapids, MI: Masters Press, 1991); Benjamin G. Rader, *Baseball: A History of America's Game* (Urbana: University of Illinois Press, 1992); Rob Ruck, *The Tropic of Baseball: Baseball in the Dominican Republic* (Westport, CT: Meckler, 1991).

2. For more on the Korean War, see Howard Zinn, *A People's History of the United States* (New York: HarperPerennial, 1980), 419–21.

3. Jonathan C. Brown, "Foreign and Native-Born Workers in Porfirian Mexico, *American Historical Review*, June 1993, 790.

4. Quoted in Rodolfo Acuña, *Occupied America: A History of Chicanos* (New York: Harper & Row, 3d ed., 1988), 116.

5. For more, see Ed Linn, *The Life and Turmoils of Ted Williams* (New York: Harcourt Brace, 1993).

6. Krich, 48.

7. Quoted in Oleksak and Oleksak, 156.

8. Quoted in Tygiel, 297.

9. All quotations from Krich, 85–86.

10. Quoted in Krich, 87.

11. Latinos won a tiny number of court victories at the local level.

For example, in 1932 a California court mandated school integration for Latinos in Lemon Grove, San Diego County, and in 1947 a similar integration decision for Latinos was won in Los Angeles County. For the full story, see James D. Cockcroft, *Latinos in the Struggle for Equal Education* (New York: Franklin Watts, 1995).

12. Quoted in Tygiel, 319.
13. Quoted in Gilbert, 25.
14. Ibid., 29–30.
15. Ibid., 33.
16. Quoted in Krich, 157.
17. Quoted in Gilbert, 52.
18. Ibid., 58.
19. Ibid., 64–65.
20. Quoted in Krich, 98.
21. Quoted in Gilbert, 83–84.
22. Ibid., 25.
23. Ibid., 103.
24. Quoted in Krich, 40.
25. Quoted in Gilbert, 102.
26. Ibid., 98.
27. Quoted in Gilbert, 100.

CHAPTER 6

1. Rod Carew, with Ira Berkow, *Carew* (New York: Simon and Schuster, 1979), 15. Besides Carew, major sources for this chapter are Felipe Alou, with Herm Weiskopf, *Felipe Alou... My Life and Baseball* (Waco, TX: Word Books, 1967); Bruce Brown, "Cuban Baseball," *The Atlantic*, 253:6 (June 1984), 109–14; Orlando Cepeda, with Bob Markus. *High and Inside: Orlando Cepeda's Story* (South Bend, IN: Icarus Press, 1983); James D. Cockcroft, *Latin America: History, Politics, and U.S. Policy* (Chicago: Nelson-Hall, 1995); Juan Marichal, with Charles Einstein, *A Pitcher's Story* (New York: Doubleday, 1967); Michael Oleksak and Mary Adams Oleksak, *Béisbol: Latin Americans and the Grand Old Game* (Grand Rapids, MI: Masters Press, 1991); John Roseboro, with Bill Libby, *Glory Days with the Dodgers and Other Days with Others* (New York: Atheneum Press, 1978); Rob Ruck, *The Tropic of Baseball: Baseball in the Dominican Republic* (Westport, CT: Meckler, 1991).

2. Cepeda, 149.
3. Noted in Paula J. Pettavino and Geralyn Pye, *Sport in Cuba: The Diamond in the Rough* (Pittsburgh: University of Pittsburgh Press, 1994), 40–42.

4. Quoted in Art Rust, Jr., *"Get That Nigger Off the Field"* (New York: Delacorte Press, 1976), 199.

5. Quoted in Oleksak and Oleksak, 184.

6. Noted in Ruck, 110–11.

7. For more, see James D. Cockcroft, *The Hispanic Struggle for Social Justice* (New York: Franklin Watts, 1994), and Hedda Garza, *Latinas: Hispanic Women in the United States* (New York: Franklin Watts, 1994).

8. Seeing the success of players' unionization and collective bargaining, umpires got in on the act too. Strikes by the Major League Umpires Association in 1970, 1979, 1984, and 1995 won them long-overdue respect and some improved pay.

9. Owners scarcely felt these penalties. Attendance was on the rise—from 45 to 55 million between 1982 and 1990—and TV and advertising revenues were going through the roof.

10. Quoted in Dan Gutman, *Baseball Babylon* (New York: Penguin Books, 1992), 352.

11. Noted in Rust, 214.

12. Ibid.

13. Brown, 110.

14. Quoted in Oleksak and Oleksak, 136.

15. Ibid.

16. Ibid.

17. Ibid.

18. Ibid.

19. Quoted in Ruck, 8.

20. Ibid.

21. Quoted in Marichal, 89.

22. Quoted in Alan M. Klein, "Culture, Politics, and Baseball in the Dominican Republic," *Latin American Perspectives*, 22:3 (Summer 1995), 116.

23. Quoted in Marichal, 162.

24. Ibid., 174. On the same page of his autobiography, Marichal claimed he never saw "racial dissension on the Giants—under Dark or under anybody else."

25. Cepeda, 33, 43.

26. Cepeda, 35.

27. A postretirement arrest and jail sentence for being found with some marijuana in his suitcase at the San Juan airport may have cost Orlando Cepeda a chance to be elected to the Hall of Fame. But he went on to become a strong voice in the campaign against drug abuse, and may yet be elected to the Hall. There have been far worse drug scandals in baseball since Cepeda's time.

28. Ali's often quoted words became the title of an award-winning documentary film in the late 1960s that showed the growing mobilization of African Americans against the war.

29. Marichal, 176.

30. Noted in *Time* magazine, June 10, 1966, 92. For more on the U.S. intervention in the Dominican Republic, see Cockcroft, *Latin America*, Chapter 10.

31. For examples, see Richard Scheinin, *Field of Screams: The Dark Underside of America's National Pastime* (New York: Norton, 1994).

32. Roseboro, 6.

33. The next season, Marichal would outhit Mays with men in scoring position, compiling a remarkable .524 average in such situations, compared with Mays's .358.

34. Roseboro, 5.

35. Quoted in Ruck, 81.

36. Roseboro, 6–7.

37. Ibid., 10. After the incident, Roseboro went on to become a famous defensive catcher, batting only .249 lifetime. He later concluded the incident had harmed both himself and Marichal, since that seemed to be all they were known for. At an old-timers' game in 1976 they finally shook hands in front of the press, although Roseboro joked "maybe we shouldn't because now they wouldn't have anything to write about" (Roseboro, 11).

38. Marichal, 186.

39. Roseboro, 10.

40. Oleksak and Oleksak, 82.

41. Quoted in Ruck, 79.

42. Marichal, 51.

CHAPTER 7

1. Quoted in John Krich, *El Béisbol: Travels through the Pan-American Pastime*, (New York: Atlantic Monthly Press, 1990), 175. This chapter is based largely on Krich, plus Bruce Brown, "Cuban Baseball," *The Atlantic*, 253:6 (June 1984), 109–14; James D. Cockcroft, *Latin America: History, Politics, and U.S. Policy* (Chicago: Nelson-Hall, 1995); Michael Oleksak and Mary Adams Oleksak, *Béisbol: Latin Americans and the Grand Old Game* (Grand Rapids, MI: Masters Press, 1991); Paula J. Pettavino and Geralyn Pye, *Sport in Cuba: The Diamond in the Rough* (Pittsburgh: University of Pittsburgh Press, 1994); Rob Ruck, *The Tropic of Baseball: Baseball in the Dominican Republic* (Westport, CT: Meckler, 1991); Howard Senzel, *Baseball and the Cold War: Being a Soliloquy on the Necessity of Baseball* (New York: Harcourt

Brace Jovanovich, 1977); Luis Tiant and Joe Fitzgerald, *El Tiante, the Luis Tiant Story* (New York: Doubleday, 1976).

2. Quoted in Krich, 223.

3. Cuba had been admitted to the IL in 1954 after its Havana Cubans of the Florida International League (see chapter 4) had led the Florida league in attendance and won four season titles and two playoff championships. In twelve years of the Caribbean World Series (see chapter 5), including the February 1960 games, Cuba won seven titles, going undefeated in three of them. After 1960, the Caribbean World Series survived without Cuba, but not too well. In 1990 its promoters moved it to Miami for three years, hoping to cash in on the large Cuban and Nicaraguan exile communities there.

4. The words attributed to Castro are from Pettavino and Pye, 42. During an ABC interview in 1991, Castro neither confirmed nor denied this bit of baseball lore that so radically altered world—and baseball—history.

5. Quoted in Senzel, 81.

6. Oleksak and Oleksak, 76.

7. After moving with the Sugar Kings from Havana to Jersey City, Cuellar banged around in the minors for most of his playing days until Houston gave him a chance. Houston traded Cuellar to Baltimore, where, starting out at age 32, he won 125 games in a six-year stretch for the Orioles (1969–74). Cuellar, Jim Palmer, and Dave McNally formed the best pitching staff around at the time. The Orioles won five division titles, three pennants, and one World Series.

8. Quoted in Oleksak and Oleksak, 125.

9. Ibid., 145.

10. Forced into exile from Cuba because of his opposition to the U.S.-backed dictatorship of Fulgencio Batista (1933–59), Dihigo had gone to Mexico City, where he met a man he later described as a "smiling young man in a Prussian-blue suit," Argentine medical doctor Ernesto "Che" Guevara. Dihigo had lent financial support for the famed rebel invasion of Batista's Cuba in 1957, when Che Guevara, Fidel Castro, and several others set sail from Mexico on the rickety boat *Granma*.

11. Pettavino and Pye, 9.

12. Quoted in Pettavino and Pye, 96.

13. Ibid., 15.

14. Pettavino and Pye, 18.

15. With the success of Cuban athletes in baseball, boxing, track and field, and other sports internationally, there have occurred the inevitable charges of use of steroids. In the very few documented instances, Cuban officials have promptly banned the athletes involved. Drug abuse is a major crime in Cuba, and there is little of it.

16. Quoted in Pettavino and Pye, 178.

17. Ibid., 162.

18. North was a gung-ho Marine who had once appeared on U.S. national TV to defend the infamous My Lai massacre in the Vietnam War. At My Lai village, all the women, children, and old people had been captured and then executed by U.S. troops and dumped in a ditch.

19. Pettavino and Pye, 40.

Chapter 8

1. Bowman and Zoss, 132. This chapter's main sources include Bowman and Zoss; S. H. Burchard, *Sports Star: Fernando Valenzuela* (San Diego: Harcourt Brace Jovanovich, 1982); John Krich, *El Béisbol: Travels through the Pan-American Pastime* (New York: Atlantic Monthly Press, 1990); Michael Oleksak and Mary Adams Oleksak, *Béisbol: Latin Americans and the Grand Old Game* (Grand Rapids, MI: Masters Press, 1991); Ken Rappaport, *Bobby Bonilla* (New York: Walker and Company, 1993); Rob Ruck, *The Tropic of Baseball: Baseball in the Dominican Republic* (Westport, CT: Meckler, 1991).

2. Krich, 117.

3. Quoted in Ruck, 178. In the 1980s, after its initial investment had multiplied tenfold, G&W sold its La Romana properties to a Cuban exile family in Miami. Naturally, the new owners continued to encourage baseball at La Romana.

4. Quoted in Ruck, 158.

5. Ibid., 47–48.

6. Ruck, 60.

7. Historically, of the more than five hundred Latinos to have played in the major leagues by 1990, about one fourth of them came from Cuba, another fourth from Puerto Rico, and another fourth from the Dominican Republic. Most of the final fourth came from Colombia, Honduras, Mexico, Nicaragua, Panama, and Venezuela.

8. Noted in Alan M. Klein, "Culture, Politics, and Baseball in the Dominican Republic," *Latin American Perspectives*, 22:3 (Summer 1995), 118.

9. For more, see Milton Jamail, "Major League Bucks," *Hispanic*, April 1993, 28.

10. Quoted in Oleksak and Oleksak, 163.

11. For more, see Hedda Garza, *Latinas: Hispanic Women in the United States* (New York: Franklin Watts, 1994), 106, 121–26.

12. Rappaport, 12.

13. Quoted in Rappaport, 58.

14. Ibid., 91.

15. Ibid., 93.

CHAPTER 9

1. John S. Bowman and Joel Zoss, *Diamonds in the Rough: The Untold History of Baseball* (New York: Macmillan, 1989), 132. Besides Bowman and Zoss, this chapter draws on Dan Gutman, *Baseball Babylon* (New York: Penguin Books, 1992); Leonard Koppett, *The New Thinking Fan's Guide to Baseball* (New York: Simon and Schuster, 1991); Michael Oleksak and Mary Adams Oleksak, *Béisbol: Latin Americans and the Grand Old Game* (Grand Rapids, MI: Masters Press, 1991); Benjamin G. Rader, *Baseball: A History of America's Game* (Urbana: University of Illinois Press, 1992); and Andrew Zimbalist, *Baseball and Billions* (New York: Basic Books, 1992).

2. Noted in Rob Ruck, *The Tropic of Baseball: Baseball in the Dominican Republic* (Westport, CT: Meckler, 1991), 85. See also Alan M. Klein, "Culture, Politics, and Baseball in the Dominican Republic," *Latin American Perspectives*, 22:3 (Summer 1995), 119.

3. Oleksak and Oleksak, 215.

4. For more on the migrant worker and immigration issues, see "Sanctions against Legal Immigrants," *Hispanic*, June 1995, 10, and James D. Cockcroft, *Latinos in the Making of the United States* (New York: Franklin Watts, 1995), Chapters 1, 3, and 6.

5. Quoted in Gutman, 332–33.

6. Quoted in Mike Bass, *Marge Schott Unleashed* (Champaign, IL: Sagamore Publishing, 1993).

7. The owners had fired Commissioner Fay Vincent because he had favored negotiating with the players' union. The owners used baseball's antitrust exemption to try to dictate to the players instead of bargain with them. Vincent later wrote: "The answer has seemed clear to me for some time. The owners and players must recapitalize the baseball business with players getting shares in the equity and future growth of the game"—Fay Vincent, "What Baseball Needs," *New York Times*, April 4, 1995.

8. For the full text of the decision, see Bass, 287–88.

9. For more, see Bass, 295–309.

10. Bob Carroll, *Baseball Between the Lies: The Hype, Hokum, and Humbug of America's Favorite Pastime* (New York: Perigee, 1993), 220.

11. The major leagues hired the first black umpire in 1965, the first black manager in 1974 (Frank Robinson).

12. Latinos became field managers long before blacks did—Mike González in the 1930s and Al López in the 1950s (see chapter 1). Preston Gómez, the Cuban shortstop imported by the Senators during World War II, later became a National League manager at San Diego (1969–73), Houston (1974–75), and Chicago (1980). Another Cuban infielder, Cookie Rojas, managed the California Angels for a

while after his late 1970s retirement from playing. But few others have reached the managerial level, even though Latino baseball savvy is by now legendary and Felipe Alou was named Manager of the Year in 1994.

13. Quoted in Gutman, 337.

14. For more on the issue of racial discrimination in baseball, see Lawrence Kahn, "Discrimination in Professional Sports," *Industrial and Labor Relations Review*, 44:3 (April 1991).

15. The Major League Baseball Players Association was founded in 1953–54 as the successor to the American Baseball Guild of 1946 that won the players' first ($5,000) minimum salary and pension plan (see chapter 5).

16. Allen St. John, "The Payoff Pitch," *Village Voice*, March 7, 1995.

17. Kevin Baker, "Ballplayers Are Workers, Too," *New York Times*, February 10, 1995.

18. Quoted in Rader, 216. In 1995, Anderson was one of the few managers who supported his players by refusing to manage the replacement players during the strike.

19. The 1962 San Francisco Giants had started the pattern of Latinos helping to bring more victories. In the 1970s the great Oakland and Cincinnati teams, with players like Tony Pérez, Dave Concepción, and Bert Campaneris, kept the Latino beat going. The 1979 World Champion Pittsburgh Pirates had a starting lineup that was half-Latino. In 1991 the Texas Rangers fielded a Latino-dominant team that included top hitters Julio Franco (Dominican Republic), Juan González (Puerto Rico), Ruben Sierra (Puerto Rico), and Rafael Palmeíro (Cuba). The 1992 World Champion Toronto Blue Jays featured Dominican pitcher Juan Guzmán and infielder Manny Lee, as well as Puerto Rican greats Roberto Alomar and Candy Maldonado.

20. By 1990 one-fifth of the ballplayers in the entire Los Angeles Dodgers system were Latino. The Dodgers' Dominican Republic "Las Palmas" complex was a "state-of-the-art" baseball school. As Philadelphia Phillies general manager Lee Thomas said: "Now we have only five to seven minor league teams apiece, and the emphasis is on teaching" (quoted in Rader, 208).

21. Quoted in Rader, 174.

22. Quoted in Gutman, 336. Batting champion Rod Carew viewed Griffith as a racist (see chapter 6).

BIBLIOGRAPHY

Alou, Felipe, with Herm Weiskopf. *Felipe Alou... My Life and Baseball*. Waco, TX: Word Books, 1967.

Bowman, John S., and Joel Zoss. *Diamonds in the Rough: The Untold History of Baseball*. New York: Macmillan, 1989.

Burchard, S. H. *Sports Star: Fernando Valenzuela*. San Diego: Harcourt Brace Jovanovich, 1982.

Burns, Ken, and Geoffrey C. Ward. *Baseball: An Illustrated History*. New York: Knopf, 1994.

Carew, Rod, with Ira Berkow. *Carew*. New York: Simon and Schuster, 1979.

Carroll, Bob. *Baseball Between the Lies: The Hype, Hokum, and Humbug of America's Favorite Pastime*. New York: Perigee, 1993.

Cepeda, Orlando, with Bob Markus. *High and Inside: Orlando Cepeda's Story*. South Bend, IN: Icarus Press, 1983.

Cockcroft, James D. *The Hispanic Struggle for Social Justice*. New York: Franklin Watts, 1994.

Garza, Hedda. *African Americans and Jewish Americans*. New York: Franklin Watts, 1995.

Gilbert, Thomas W. *Roberto Clemente*. New York: Chelsea House, 1991.

Gilbert Tom. *Baseball and the Color Line*. New York: Franklin Watts, 1995.

Gutman, Dan. *Baseball Babylon*. New York: Penguin Books, 1992.

Hollander, Zander, ed. *1995 The Complete Handbook of Baseball*. New York: Signet, 1995.

Klein, Alan M. *Sugarball: The American Game, the Dominican Dream*. New Haven, CT: Yale University Press, 1991.

Koppett, Leonard. *The New Thinking Fan's Guide to Baseball*. New York: Simon and Schuster, 1991.

Krich, John. *El Béisbol: Travels through the Pan-American Pastime*. New York: Atlantic Monthly Press, 1990.

Margolies, Jacob. *The Negro Leagues: The Story of Black Baseball*. New York: Franklin Watts, 1993.

Marichal, Juan, with Charles Einstein. *A Pitcher's Story*. New York: Doubleday, 1967.

Miñoso, Orestes, and Fernando Fernandez and Robert Kleinfelder. *Extra Innings: My Life in Baseball*. Chicago: Regnery Gateway, 1983.

Gilbert, Tom. *Baseball and the Color Line*. New York: Franklin Watts, 1995.

Oleksak, Michael, and Mary Adams Oleksak. *Béisbol: Latin Americans and the Grand Old Game*. Grand Rapids, MI: Masters Press, 1991.

Peterson, Robert. *Only the Ball Was White*. New York: McGraw-Hill, 1970.

Pettavino, Paula J., and Geralyn Pye. *Sport in Cuba: The Diamond in the Rough*. Pittsburgh: University of Pittsburgh Press, 1994.

Rappaport, Ken. *Bobby Bonilla*. New York: Walker and Company, 1993.

Rader, Benjamin G. *Baseball: A History of America's Game*. Urbana: University of Illinois Press, 1992.

Rogosin, Donn. *Invisible Men: Life in Baseball's Negro Leagues*. New York: Atheneum, 1983.

Ruck, Rob. *The Tropic of Baseball: Baseball in the Dominican Republic*. Westport, CT: Meckler, 1991.

Tiant, Luis, and Joe Fitzgerald. *El Tiante, the Luis Tiant Story*. New York: Doubleday, 1976.

Tygiel, Jules. *Baseball's Great Experiment: Jackie Robinson and His Legacy*. New York: Oxford University Press, 1983.

Zimbalist, Andrew. *Baseball and Billions*. New York: Basic Books, 1992.

INDEX

Page numbers in *italics* refer to illustrations.